Learning Hosea's Song

A Novel Modern Commentary on the Book of Hosea

By

Lewis E. Miles

ISBN: 0-7596-8642-4

This book is printed on acid free paper.

1stBooks - rev. 02/25/02

PREFACE

The book of Hosea is one part of the Bible which has long fascinated me. My curiosity about what is not stated, but is perhaps implied, has provided the motivation for me to produce this story, using poetry, prose, and references from various parts of the Bible.

My late father-in-law encouraged me to record the products of the stirrings of my curiosity. He suggested that I use his name and the names of others who don't protest the idea to help me get into projecting the "voice" of the main character. He also suggested using a chronology parallel to my own.

While I am aware of the possibility that some readers might find this work to be far from their expectations for historical fiction, that is not my main concern.. However you perceive it, if this work prompts you to think, to meditate, to study the scriptures, or to pray, my goal will have been reached.

Now the time has come for me to become silent so the voice of the character of the story can be heard.

Lewis E. Miles

The dates at the end of each poem are the dates of composition, if known. Dates in parenthesis are the chronology of the story.

DEDICATION

This work
is dedicated
to each
and every one
who desires
to become
part of the group
which fulfills
our Lord's command,
"be ye therefore
wise as serpents
and
harmless as doves."

TABLE OF CONTENTS

FOREWORD

She was a quite compliant child,
Although she surely acted wild.
She was doing as she'd been taught;
No other vision had she caught.
Her name we do not even know—
The streets her handle did bestow.
"Intensity", one might well say,
Earned her handle in the sad fray.

With Moses' laws he is not slack—
Shew Bread in its place he would stack.
A pious man might some think he,
But through the moonlight others see
Him heading for the groves of Baal,
Leading his daughter without fail.

Hey "Two Cakes", have we got a plan!
She'll never settle with one man.
We'll torment her 'til hope is numb—
Forever to our grove she'll come!

Great! Fellows, I do like the plan!
She'll make me a powerful man.
The priests will see that I'm blessed,
'Cause my alter girl is the best!

A sound of gossip by the gate
~~~ a "reputation" at age eight.
You don't say! Well, it is a shame.
A reproach on the fam'ly name.
~~~ he believes in her salvation.
~~~ she'll just bring him ruination.

But God had spoken to His friend,
Go show her kindness without end.
A man of sorrow, and of grief,
Steadfast through troubles past belief.
Through years of sorrow they will come,
Beaten down, but not overcome.

A sound of gossip by the gate—
~~~ don't think she'll ever get things straight.
~~~ wears his ring and uses his name,
Yet his religion does not claim.

Come be depressed for many days;
Come muck through sorrow's fearsome maze.
That's what I read in Chapter Three,
Mr. Salvation's litany.

Like a freight train, loaded and long,
Comes forth the sorrow of life's song.
Don't hope to shorten her grief time;
Can't stop that freight train on a dime.

Her man of sorrows and of grief
From his torment found no relief.
When Rachel lost her children,
He was there, midst scenes so bewild'ren,
Too much in shock to even cry,
Or even stop to question why.

A sound of gossip by the gate.
We told him he was tempting fate.
~~~ tried to tell that Salvation clown
That girl would surely bring him down.
I think he's got a heart of stone—
Can even God for him attone?
Well, even stone will someday break.
~~~ his "helping her" is a mistake.

When years have stretched his sorrows long,
In his head still rings Rachel's song.
Dear Lord, you've been a friend to me,
Helping me face reality.
From life's path I don't wish to flee,

But how long is my chapter three?
How long 'til people understan'
Grief is part of redemption's plan?

A sound of gossip by the gate.
Looks like they're giving up of late.
She never darkens the church door.
~~~ took her name from the books for shore.
He says we should leave her alone,
Since we don't like to hear her moan.
He sits alone and looks so glum—
Why does he even bother to come?
~~~ might have known their destination.
~~~ said she'd bring him ruination.

His prayers go up to Heaven's court.
Lord, heed not their evil report.
~~~ them not fall in sight of the prize.
I pray, o Lord, open their eyes.
Show them the hidden mystery;
Help them understand chapter three.

8 / 18,19,& 26 / 1998

FOCUS

Though I speak with tongues of men and angels
but dare not face the truth,

If I keep the Lord's Sabbath holy
to my old age from my youth,

But hide in my heart my darkest secrets,
hiding from the whole truth,

I will never enter the Kingdom
of the Author of truth.

But I need not tremble with terror,
or to faint, full of fright;

Redeeming us is His greatest mission,
blessing us His delight.

He will surely help me open my heart,
show me the hidden key,

For He is the great and loving giver
of life and liberty

10/16/92

For precept must be upon precept, precept upon precept; line upon line, line upon line; here a little and there a little; For with stammering lips and another tongue will he speak to this people. Isaiah 28:10&11.

xiii

Section One

Early Lessons

SHOPPING WITH GRANDMA

I'm making a grocery list;
Would you like to help me?
You always add a humorous twist.
To help grandma I did agree.

I thought it a funny caper
To come up with crazy things
Like soap or toilet paper,
Or popcorn and onion rings.

I think that will have to do,
She would eventually say.
Come along if you're going to,
I haven't got all day.

Then we'd get in her car
And she'd crank it up to go,
But we'd never get that far,
For she worried so.

What am I forgetting?
I know there must be more.
Can't you think of something
We haven't mentioned before?

Oh yes, I know something
That we really need.
I always keep forgetting
To bring home more bird seed.

We go to the store.
She doesn't use the list,
So I have to remind her,
If you get the gist.

To the garage will you take this?
I'm afraid I'll see a mouse.
The seed goes on a stack which doesn't exist,
Then I run back to the house.

11/14/93

This grandma had been mistreated as a youngster, a fact I came to understand as a preschooler. Although my grandfather never told me much about the details, when I was older he told me that childhood sexual abuse was behind her strange adult behavior. This set of grandparents was kind and generous, and what I learned from them helped me deal with the mistreatment I received from my other grandfather.

I TOLD

Young was I, and innocent,
Knowing naught of grandpa's bent.
Warming myself by the stove,
Heard a commotion up above,
And glanced up through the grate.
(Spider webs adorned the grate)
To protest indeed had she cause,
For someone else's wife she was.
He taunted her before the attack—
Naked into the corner she'd back'd.
A sound like jumping on a bed.
Said she, I'd rather I were dead.

When they had come downstairs,
I gave him my hardest glares.
Don't stare, boy, ya know its rude.
Not as rude as you are crude.
He said I didn't know crude,
So the following I spewed;

Spider webs between her legs—
She's afraid of rubber pegs.
You say it is just great,
But I see hell through the grate.

Some say I killed my king that day;
I stabbed him with my verse.
The judges found me innocent,
But my punishment got much worse.
He said that I was terrible—
"That kid is a big disgrace."
I said he was a F.A.T. liar,
And I said it to his face.
He said, "I'm gonna whip you!"
I said, "You wanna bet?"
"How are you gonna stop me?"
"Don't touch me; my dad'll kill you yet." *

"I'll not sit at the table with him any more;
He throws ketchup on the ceiling and ice cream on the floor."
He got up from the table, looking very sore.
"Well, he's a messy eater, if you know what that means;
Every time he comes here, he always dumps the beans.

I knew why she'd been screaming; he was out of place.
I told him if he touched me, I'd spit right in his face.
Yes, I killed my tyrant then, ere I finished school.
Though he lived for many years, he lived on as a fool.

1/26/93 & 4/19/2001

*He knew I gave reference to a man I'd conversed with on the telephone, not my father. The gangster had called me son, and had told grandpa that if he ever heard I'd spit in his face, he was as good as dead.

TWO WAY STREET

Took a message for Bignose Fred;
This is what the Lone Ranger said,
"Wash your feet 'fore you go to bed,
Or we'll come fill your sheets with lead."

He insisted we went for a walk,
But I wouldn't stop my talk:
You've not for your safety very well planned—
They've been tracin' your tracks in the sand.
They're measurin' 'em for the size of your feet,
And you won't get help from the man up the street.
You'd best hurry up and pay your dues,
Unless you like wearing concrete shoes.

You think I can't brush out my tracks,
But I know about weeds and gunny sacks.
I'll just break off this ol' milkweed;
It is just about what I need.
Backwards up the driveway he went,
His posture not the only thing bent.
I couldn't quite contain my glee
As I called out merrily,
I think you'd best look out,
Or you'll add to your reasons to pout,
But he backed right into the thistle's spine:
It was a sight I thought most fine!
Oh! Look what you made me do!
I ought to show you a point or two.
I was laughing so at his surprise
That tears were running from my eyes.
Ha! Just a little fun it did poke;
Can't you even take a joke?

7/1 & 11/29/93

Although I was only ten years old, I had already confronted him about his sexual abuse of some of the members of the family. His response was to assault me. I knew he was somehow involved in dealings with gangsters from Chicago, and that he was more afraid of them than he let on. When I happened to answer the call from one of them warning him to pay up, I decided to see if those men would defend me against him somehow. I told the man who had called I'd tell him something, and that he would find out what it was when his man reported to him. Oh yes, I exclaimed, may I ask who called? You can call me Joe Bananas, he replied, and don't forget.

When grandpa got home, he found the note. He was angry, but worried too. I agreed to walk to the mailbox with him on the condition that he wouldn't touch me. His efforts to "reason with" me consisted entirely of trying to get me to agree with his minimizing and denial. He became angry when I not only refused to go along with his ideas, but also added to his fears about the mob. His temper tantrum gave me a good opportunity to turn some of his frequently used words of dismissal when accused into something to make fun of his predicament and make sure he understood I was declaring that he had brought it on himself by his own foolish choices.

Questions those men asked me in subsequent calls opened up the secrets of his abuse of his own family.

After making sure I understood the seriousness of any such actions on my part, they told me that as a last resort self defense if he wouldn't back off, to spit in his face. That, they said, would be the kiss of Judas if they found out about it. They made sure he knew what they'd told me, too.

Chronologically the preceding events came before the ones portrayed in I Told, but I decided to present them in the order family and friends might have discovered them. As is often the case, many chose not to see what was going on, or to pretend there was nothing they could do personally to stop or restrain grandpa.

*   *   *   *   *   *   *   *   *   *   *   *   *   *   *   *   *   *   **   *   *   *   **   *   *   *

AN OBSERVATION

They say truth is stranger than fiction;

Can you second that with conviction?

Though some will say this story's untrue,

And others that over nothing I make ado,

Why I'd imagine such misery

Is to me a great mystery.

These few tales are but a part

Of the woes of grieving hearts,

For I know he hurt others too,

And each of those suffers too.

12/1/93

A WORD OF CAUTION

There are a few things I should tell you, son;

Life for me has not been much fun.

I'm not just the man from down the street:

I'm over 'bout everyone you meet.

Don't let anyone tell you how to run your life,

But don't be stirrin' up extra strife;

Let your conscience be your guide,

Or you will curl up and die inside.

No, I'll not tell you how your life's to be spent,

But please don't follow Bignose' bent.

"Roarin' Lion" Leo
@ 1966

He was an extended family member for one of my cousins, and lived not far from my mean grandfather. He had gotten involved with the mob through a labor union, and had invited grandpa to join him before he fully understood what he was involved with. He told me he wished he could get out, but couldn't figure out how to get them to let him. When I asked him why he recited the poem to me, he wanted to make sure I knew

that what he and grandpa were involved with was not all fun and games. He needn't have worried about that—I was decidedly against grandpa's drug dealing, as well as his sexual violence. I was simply looking for protection and power to defend myself and others from his abuse. I found out that even these organized crime bosses didn't care to tolerate such behavior. I decided to use that knowledge as a tool to slow him down, or even perhaps get him to repent and change his ways.

When "Roarin' Lion" Leo died, he was still trying to figure out to get them to let him out before he retired or died. I remember feeling angry that he had died instead of grandpa. I resolved to never forget what he had told me that day on the telephone.

Section Two

Conversations with Walter

Lewis E. Miles

Walter was a special friend
From early in my youth.
I could tell him everything
When others feared the truth.

He asked about my sleeping bag
And who joined me one night;
Although my words made others gag,
He said I might be right.

I said, Other boys see a prostitute
And brag about their fun,
But I see value absolute,
And a life that's just begun.

I believe you, and I'll help you out,
But don't tell anyone.
Blind and evil hearted folks
Would believe you did it just for fun.

We talked about the difference
Between taking a prostitute or a wife,
How it is a firm commitment
To stick with her for life.

He could have really hurt me;
He could have taken her away,
But he just said tenderly,
Your time will come some day.

****

We talked about an orchard,
And what guys did for "fun".
He said to me, Tread gently,
Your battle's just begun.

Lately, he said, I've been discouraged;
I've thought I've failed at life,
For I can't seem to keep up
With my roving wife.

Treat her as kindly, said I,
As you would if she was very sick,
For she's drunk the wine of harlotry,
And her confusion's very thick.

She received the habit early,
Perhaps as a young child,
And it would take a miracle
To keep her from acting wild.

Compare the book of Hosea
With Revelation seventeen,
And you will see a picture
Many preachers haven't seen.

He thanked me for my advice,
And then gave some to me.
Don't stop when things get difficult,
Or be too quick to flee.

When Moses said to Pharaoh,
I AM said, Let my people go,
Pharaoh didn't slack up a bit—
He gave them a harder row to hoe.

Don't give up just because
Life gets much worse for her;
God will free her in His own time,
Of that you can be sure.

****

Much hotter grew the battle
As life stepped up the pace.
He offered me encouragement
That helped me hardships face.

When events overloaded me,
And I forgot somehow,
He quietly came and spoke to me,
Reminding me of my vow.

****

You are my favorite outlaw,
He teased me many a time,
And he often greeted me
With a riddle or a rhyme.

Who did you come to see today,
My daughter or your wife?
That is something I couldn't say;
A lot depends on her.
Her understanding isn't clear—

11

Her lines are thin and blurred.
You needn't think I'll condemn you
For living a double life.

I thought our words were private,
But someone overheard.
If you don't mind me interrupting,
I'd like to say a word.

It's really none of your business.
I hope you've not heard everything,
But go ahead and say a word;
It can't hurt anything.

I think that what you're saying
Is really quite absurd.
Perhaps you need your glasses on
If you think her lines are blurred.
You know what I was saying,
So don't let me hear you whine.
If you try to twist my words,
You are no friend of mine.

All right, you two,
That is enough.
I don't want someone leaving
In a great big huff.

I've begun to like you;
I hope you stick around.
If you find yourself getting beaten,
I'll help you stand your ground.

****

He nodded his approval
When I did agree
That I would accompany her
To watch out for her safety.

I thought she was just worrying,
But little did I know
She wanted me to protect her
From a deadly foe.

Walter thought he was powerless,
But when I told him, No,
You can just tell everyone
That we have to go,

With that little encouragement
He quickly came to life—
Then I had to caution him
Against stirring up the strife.

Although there was an argument,
Away we quickly went:
To go his wife was not inclined—
In fact she got quite bent.

****

About that day I'll say to you—
I think you saved her life.
When do you want to take her
For your full time wife?

You needn't get so anxious,
For she is still quite young.
Now I think it's your turn
To need to hold your tongue.

You're welcome on my property
At whatever time you please,
And if they try to lock you out,
I'll make you your own keys.

You know there are others
Who will dispute your word.
"Don't ever show your face again"
Is the word I heard.

You're certainly welcome at my place,
And it's I who hold the deed,
So if they try to stop you,
Come tell me what you need.

****

The tension was quite rough on her;
I could sense she needed a break,
Then I had a chance to help
An opportunity to make.

She needs some time away from home,
And perhaps away from me,
To have some time to think
And search for reality.

To work at camp all winter
She had the opportunity.
He discussed it with me briefly,
Then to consent we did agree.

****

Events soon ran together.
And life became a blur.
Every now and then he'd ask me,
How long will you wait for her?

Then one day she and I talked,
And set a wedding date,
But that frightened her too much;
She said she couldn't wait.

Once again I took her,
And she conceived a child.
When we told her parents,
Her mother plain went wild.

Walter stood up to his wife,
And said, What's done is done.
You've no right to threaten
Her or him or anyone.

When things had settled down
He talked with me a bit.
I sure am thankful
You didn't give up and quit.

You have long been learning
To sing Hosea's song.
I have one clear question—
Why did you wait so long?

Because I wouldn't take her
Until it was her will.
A woman convinced against her will
Is of the same opinion still,

And though I remember you gave me
The right to claim her as mine,
I would not stoop to force her—
Freedom of choice is a right divine.

****

Many years came and went
Until his life was nearly spent.
The last few words he spoke to me
Were a deep compliment.

I don't see how you
Have put up with all of us.
Just to think about it
Is enough to make me cuss.

A little understanding
Was really all it took,
For God gave us all the answers
Recorded in the Holy Book.

I wish you'd take my Bible
And mark it with a pen,
Or at least tell me where you learned
What you told me back then,

For seldom is an old man
Instructed by a boy,
But you were a wise man
Whose company I did enjoy.

I cannot mark your Bible,
Nor can I make a list,
But I'll tell you what I studied;
I think you'll get the gist.

I read the books of Moses,
Especially the laws,
And searched in the New Testament
To learn what Jesus saw.

■■■■■■■■■■■■■■■■■■■■■■■■■■■■■■■■■■

As I look back on his life,
I can see he was my friend.
If I had it to do over,
More time with him I'd spend,

For he knew my deepest heartaches,
And let me know he cared.
It means a lot to remember
Some of the words we shared.

Some thought he was crazy;
They even said as much
When he asked about newspapers,
And why I cried so much.

Do you ever read Ann Landers,
Or do you still sit and cry?
Her sister's name was the problem;
Sometimes my eyes still won't stay dry.

Her grandma sure was crazy;
There just was no excuse.
I tried to reason with her,
But my effort was no use.

You know that wasn't her first,
Although her first by me.
I'd have loved Benoni
And treasured all his glee,

But if I'd had to give him up,
That would I have done;
He'd have been to someone
A precious little son.

We had a lot in common,
I think you will agree.
'Tis sad that what links us
Is our pain and misery.

The things we discussed together
When no one else would hear
Were why he knew my sorrow
And why I knew his grief and fear.

1993

This poem is a tribute to a friend who had the courage to look beyond his first reactions, try to understand what really would be the best thing to say or do under the circumstances, and to listen long enough to get a good comprehension of where a young person's heart and head were really focused.

One day at school in September of 1968, I got permission to leave the classroom to go to the restroom. As I entered the corridor which contained the entrance to the boy's room, a small boy ran past. He exited the building and kept right on running, across the street and behind another building. I ran after him to find out where he was going and why he was running away like that. He had run because he was frightened.

He thought he would get whipped for forgetting instructions on behavior. I convinced him that the teachers wouldn't beat him, and he went back to the school with a teacher's aide who had also seen him run.

The teachers were easy to convince that the boy needed encouragement, not punishment, because in the few days which had already passed in that school year, I had already discovered that terror, not defiance, was what motivated another lower grade boy to take off from lineup and go hide. His caregivers had been confronted about beating him, and his behavior had steadily improved.

These episodes preceding September 23 were why I was called to help find a third grade girl who had disappeared during recess. Some girls from my seventh grade class and some eighth grade girls were also asked to help the teachers and teacher's aides find her. Someone found her hiding under a bridge over the creek, but she wouldn't come out, and hadn't said why. I was asked to go try to talk to her. Eventually she told me she was "Afraid of that man." The teachers and I understood this to mean sexual abuse, and the man who had been walking past when she ran and hid was ordered to stay off the school grounds.

When Walter discovered that this man was undeterred, and only waited for her to get out of school for the day to intercept her down the street, he knew he had to do something. After talking with the teachers from the school, he spent some time talking with me, then asked me to help keep track of her after school.

Thus began several years of cooperation to try to help the girl some said was the wildest, craziest, most mixed up girl they knew; one they figured would never settle down. While some saw that as reason to write her off, others understood that texts like Matthew 7:12, Matthew 25: 40, and Acts 20:35 are instructions on how to treat the least promising, weakest, and most confused individuals.

Walter and I sometimes got on each other's nerves, and occasionally provoked the other to anger, as is the case in most friendships, but our mutual interest in listening and sharing advise opened the doors for a depth and intensity of friendship we greatly valued. Our last conversations were of this nature.

* * * * *

I could ask a thousand questions—why? What I can't do is answer all of them. Although I could explain some of the factors which influenced peoples decisions, there is much that is beyond our grasp.

Walter, along with others who tried to help us, made mistakes which limited how much they actually helped. Walter and others helped us more than they sometimes realized, and I am thankful for their concern and efforts. My hope is that someone can learn from this collection of writings, and that a portion of the blessing of kindness we received will be passed on to others.

* * * * *

Moreover, brethren, I would not that ye should remain ignorant, how that all our fathers were under the cloud, and all passed through the sea;... Neither murmur ye, as some of them murmured, and were destroyed of the destroyer. Now all these things happened unto them for ensamples: and they are written for our admonition, upon whom the ends of the world are come. Wherefore let him that thinketh he standeth take heed lest he fall. I speak as to wise men; judge ye what I say. I Corinthians 10:1,10-12,15.

Section Three

History or Allegory?

The Story

Lewis E. Miles

INTRODUCTIONS

What are you doing
    down here at the creek?
It's not time to
    play hide and seek.

        I don't care,
            I'm afraid of that man,
        And I'll keep
            out of his sight if I can

He walked on by
    and went up the hill
If you're afraid he'll come back,
    I don't think he will.

        He just went around front
            and he's looking for me.
        Please go up there and look;
            he's just waiting for me.

You are right;
    he did circle around,
But the teachers ordered him
    off the school grounds.
If he forgets,
    or concocts explanations,
They'll be glad to walk him
    right to the police station.
Come walk with me
    to the jungle gym;
When you're close to me,
    you needn't fear him.

7/16/93

    Although we had met and conversed before this, this event was when I learned her name and told her mine. The teachers had asked me to help find her because she had vanished during recess. Because of my success in defending myself from my grandfather, I was not afraid of this man. When he sassed the two women who intercepted him as he tried to circle around, I didn't hesitate to tell him off. I was twelve, and she was nine at the time of this incident.

19

REQUESTS

Her dad,..I want to ask you a favor,
to me   Although doing it I don't savor,
        For it pains me that my daughter
        Is being treated in ways men hadn't oughter,
        But I thank you for noticing her fear,
        And helping make the sources clear.
        Though folks may think I'm a fool,
        I'm asking you to escort her after school
        To see she arrives where she belongs
        Instead of receiving more wrongs.

My ……..Will you let me be your friend?
words   I'll try to protect you, the best I know how;
to her   On my friendship you can depend.
        If you're scared again, you know where to run now;
        Run to me if you see him again.

Her ……..When she saw him again, running she came
I   response (Hoping I'd not let his plans happen)
        Right through the infield, ignoring the game.

Slowly, surely, friendship grew.
In time I discovered other foes too,
Both the Pharisee and the publican
Who'd hard heartedly do things banned.

Said her father, with a tear in his eye,
I believe that you'll do the best that you can;
To comfort and protect her you'll really try.
Somehow I sense that you will always be her man.

1/24/94

That first meeting with her dad, which he had gotten the school teachers to set up, was an awkward, unnerving time for me, as well as for him. He mumbled, hemmed and hawed, and stumbled around for words. Finally he stopped and asked if I understood what he meant. Yes, I think I do, I replied. If you will give me a minute or two, I'll try to organize what I think you said. Take your time, he said. I've got plenty of time. A few minutes later, I said something similar to the first ten lines. We agreed that the awkward gangly poetry matched the mood of the occasion. When people criticized his decision, he simply asked them, "Do you have a better solution?"

ELEVEN

Sleep sound in Jesus, my little girl friend.
Stay right here with me clear through to the end.
Angels are watching, there's no need to fear;
They'll keep us safely for many a year.

Sleep sound in Jesus, sweetheart of my heart;
In the darkest night let us not be apart.
Come here and lie down in my bed for the night;
I'll hold you gently 'til morning is light.

Sleep sound in Jesus, come learn with me here;
We'll learn together for many a year
About salvation and eternal love,
Then we'll be ready for God's house above.

4/11/70 & 2/21/93

11th of April
11 years old her age
11 O'clock that night
May have been 11 people on the campout

This poem is probably the strangest one I ever composed, if not in content, in setting and motive. Although I was trying to compose something poetic, my idea was to compose something to calm her fears and at the same time convince her friendship was best started without sexual interaction, something she seemed not to understand. I had told her, not now, later, when she tried to insist, and told her she needed to get some sleep first. I lay there awake, telling God I thought the dreams I had repeatedly over the previous few nights were ridiculous. An angel had stood over me and told me not to turn her away. When I argued that I was too young, and not ready to take a wife, he told me that if I waited until I thought I was ready, it would be too late for her. I shook my head and prayed that the Lord would guide my thoughts, and began to compose a poem. Shocked at the first four lines, I immediately tried again, only to be just as disturbed by the next four lines. "Lord, this sounds terrible," I prayed. "I'll try one more time, so please guide me." The last four lines came quickly into my mind. I was angry. "God, why are you treating me this way?" "You promised me you would take the craziest, most mixed up girl for whom there was any hope if that is what I want you to do," His soft voice answered. "But we're too young," I protested. The only response I got was a review of my previous dreams, along with a new one that showed her stumbling off into the dark and falling over a waterfalls because I had rejected her. She woke me in the wee hours of the night, and asked me if I would do something now. I said, no we really shouldn't, or something to that effect. "But you promised," she replied. So I did, I muttered to myself, thinking again about the dreams. OK, I replied, but this is serious. You have to agree to make some promises, and really keep them. My poems of a few hours past were forgotten, not to be recollected for many years. Promise me, I said, that you will always be my friend, and that you'll run to me whenever you're afraid.

APRIL 12

You'd best forget about that girl
Though you've taken her for a whirl.
You will never settle her down,
For she's the wildest thing around.

You're all afraid of her, I said.
Well, my heart is not filled with dread,
Nor am I run by hate or spite;
I know she's valued in God's sight,
Though she's hurting, shattered and torn,
And you wish she was never born.
I see value deep down inside,
And I will have her for my bride.

Man! You don't know what that will take!
For five or ten years she will shake
You off just like you don't exist.
She'll stab your heart, then she'll twist
The knife around to ease her own pain;
You'd best not mess with her again!

I'll try again; the bitter cup
I'll drink again; I won't give up
Though it may take twenty five years,
Love will conquer all her fears,
For she too is a child of God;
Someday streets of gold she will trod,
For God is gracious and He is good.
He'll restore her to personhood,
Then she will be no longer wild;
She will walk in peace as His child.

3/20/93

This poem tells the story of what happened because I made little effort to hide the truth about what happened after she insisted sometime before daylight that I keep my promise of "later". This is not a very good start for a permanent relationship, I thought. Now it will be my responsibility to try to stop her abusers. I decided to heed the warning dreams, claim her for my wife in spite of our young age, and talk to her father about our situation. I knew the guys would be likely to taunt me, or at least to try to "warn me", but that didn't really bother me.

A BOOK OF REMEMBRANCE

We know the angel wrote above
Words of promise, words of love,
That we shared in that sodden tent
Where our very first night was spent.

Yes, said I, I did promise you
I'd do it later. I will, too,
But I must tell you something first;
For me it cannot be reversed.
If I play, it will be for keeps—
Let's talk now so nobody weeps.
Our whole future is at stake;
A word of promise each must make.

Said I, As long as we both live,
My friendship to you I will give.
Though a perfect job I can't do,
I'll do my best to protect you.

You heard the promise that I made;
Promise me that when you're afraid
You will come running straight to me.
I will be glad to, then said she.
On your protection I'll depend,
And forever I'll be your friend.

4/26/94

We both thought of writing down our promises to each other that day. More than once she looked for a pencil we had seen. The two pens the adults in charge of the campout had brought were so wet they wouldn't write.

Later, when our transportation came to evacuate us, someone offered us a writing utensil, but by then so much commotion had been raised over the events that we felt uneasy about writing anything down. We better wait and see what her father says, I answered. Besides, it is already written down. It can't be, someone objected. You already said nobody had anything to write with. That's right, I replied, but that didn't keep it from being entered into the Book of Remembrance by the angels who record everything.

Of course, neither of us is certain exactly what we said so many years ago word for word, but this poem reflects the themes of our promises to each other early that morning, before dawn.

PEACHES & SCREAMS

Narration	She's in a hurry as she goes by;
	She doesn't see me waving,
	Nor hear my cry,
My words	"Wait for me!"

Narration	Now she is running;
	How her feet fly!
	I couldn't catch her
	Even if I tried.

Boys	Come and go with us,
	We'll all have some fun.
	She won't mess around
	When we get done.

My words	What you're suggesting
	Ought not to be done;
	It won't help her or you,
	Or, for that matter, anyone.

My first	They'll never catch her,
thoughts	I said to myself,
and	And tried to put my fears
reactions	On the back shelf.

I tried to go
Right on and play.
Lingering doubts
Wouldn't go away.

What if they catch her and
And hurt her bad?
I made a promise
To her dad.

So then I turn
With a heavy heart;
Toward the mountain
I sadly start.

I met one of them
Coming back,
And heard a word
Of their attack.

A boy

She's up there,
He said with a sneer,
Acting brave
To cover his fear.

That is,
What's left of her;
I wouldn't look
If you I were.

Narration

I slipped away
Out of sight,
Then I ran
With all my might.

I caught my breath
At the top of the path,
Propped up my courage,
And held my wrath.

I stepped into the orchard
And looked around.

Boys

There's her man,
Said they, covering ground.

Narration

How many there were
I still don't know,
But their departure
Was anything but slow.

Her reaction

Oh, she cried!
You want in on it too?
Don't you know
I could whip you?

My reply

No, said I.
Can't you see,
I just made
All your foes flee?

Please tell me what
I can do for you.
Where are your clothes?
I'll get them for you.

Her response

No, please hold me,
'Cause I surely hurt,
And I need comforting
More than a shirt.

Narration	I held her and soothed her For quite a while, 'Til finally she said With a weak smile,
Her request	Will you please get me My socks and shoes, And the other things You think I could use.
Narration	I looked high and low; Most everywhere, To find all the things For her repair.

She'd been heading home,
So I took her there,
Hoping that I would
Get treated fair,

But her mother became
A hysterical mess;
To repeat what she said
Would not be best.

She would not even
Let me explain—
I was unwelcome,
She made it plain.

| Later | I talked to her father
As man to man
While he sipped the water
I'd placed in his hand. |

We talked about Hosea
And his wild wife,
Wondering if he'd
Experienced such strife.

He apologized for
His ungrateful wife,
And he called his daughter
My little wife.

Walter   I think you've proven
Quite fair and square
You'll try hard to protect her,
And that you do care.

7/16/93

A bunch of guys she'd messed with decided to get revenge for her running around and making false promises to so many guys. My disruption of their activities came as their anger and violence was getting out of hand. She was twelve, and I was fifteen. (1971)

FIREFLIES

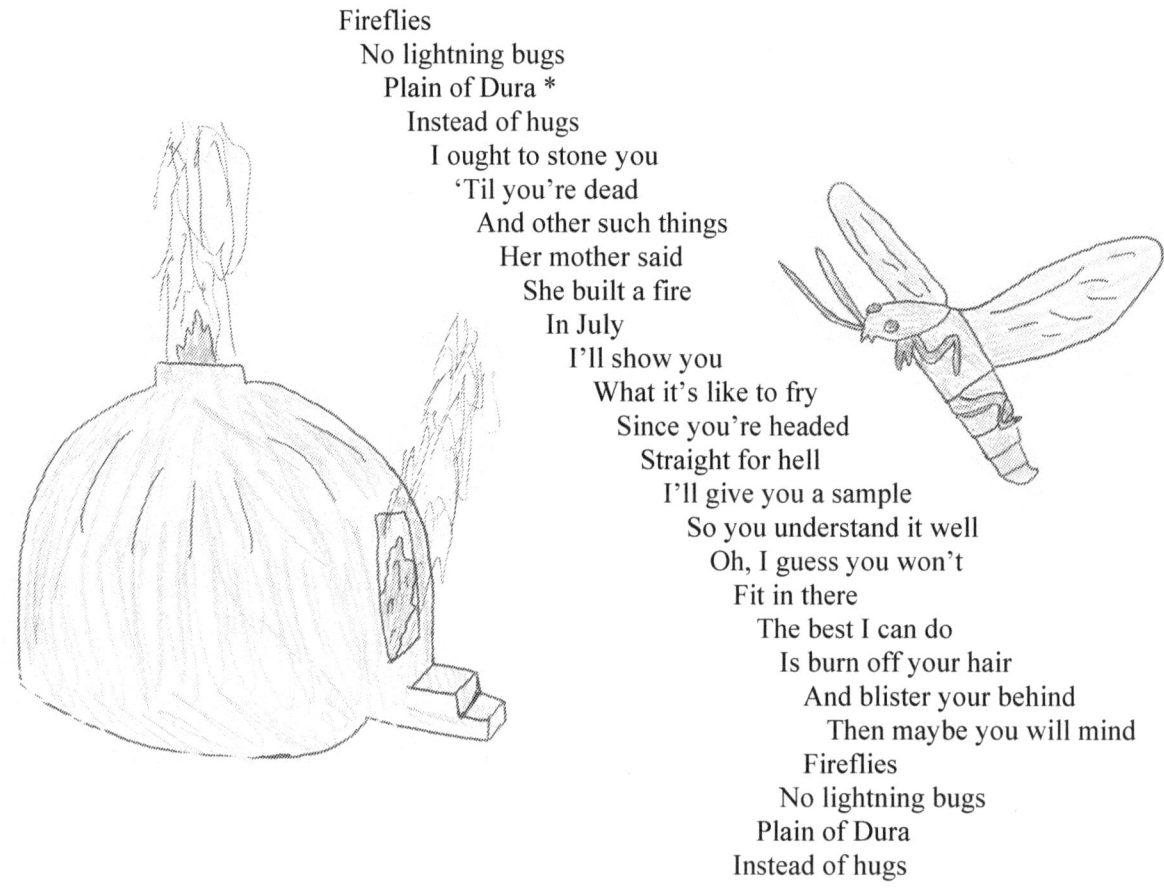

Fireflies
No lightning bugs
Plain of Dura *
Instead of hugs
I ought to stone you
'Til you're dead
And other such things
Her mother said
She built a fire
In July
I'll show you
What it's like to fry
Since you're headed
Straight for hell
I'll give you a sample
So you understand it well
Oh, I guess you won't
Fit in there
The best I can do
Is burn off your hair
And blister your behind
Then maybe you will mind
Fireflies
No lightning bugs
Plain of Dura
Instead of hugs

7/18/93

*See Daniel 3: 1, 19, & 20

This poem is a reflection on her mother's reaction to finding out about the incident in the orchard, and other related events.

___

And when his disciples James and John saw this, they said, Lord, wilt thou that we command fire to come down from heaven, and consume them, even as Elias did?

But he turned, and rebuked them, and said, Ye know not what manner of spirit ye are of.

For the Son of man is not come to destroy men's lives, but to save them. And they went to another village. Luke 9: 54—56

"HORSERADISH!"

That girl likes horses
And she's good with them too.
Come up some time;
I'll show you a thing or two.

Perhaps, said I,
Sometime I will.
I'll not make a promise
I can't fulfill.

I mistrusted him
And his horsin' around,
For he trod
On forbidden ground.

I waited my time,
Then one day
I went to see
What games he did play

He tried to include me
In doing perverted acts,
But with him
I would make no pacts.

You beastly man!
To her you hadn't oughter,
To say nothing of
Misusing your own daughters.

Get out of my house
If you won't play along.
You're not welcome here
If you must sing that song.

Yes, I'm learning
Hosea's song.
Go to jail,
Where you belong.

I went to her father
And we came back;
We then launched
A counter-attack.

Dad said to him
With forceful tone,
You better leave
His wife alone.

You can't be saying
These children are married!
To the loony bin
You need to be carried.

If they're such children,
Leave them alone.
Let them play,
Or I'll gather stones.

7/17/93

This poem tells the story of the most intense of several confrontations with the man from whom she was hiding when I first learned her name, and how her father attempted to put him in his place. At least one of them must have talked about the incident, and about her dad calling her my wife, because several people asked me if he really said that. When they asked me how he could say such a thing, I would point them to Exodus 22: 16, and ask them if they knew the difference between a wife and a concubine. Most of them couldn't give an answer, so I'd tell them that according to my understanding, a concubine was a wife with none of the legal rights which usually come automatically to a wife at marriage. (1971)

PREACHER MAN

Take her with you
I don't care;
Teach her something
If you dare
It's about time she learned
There's more to life than school
Take her, preacher, teach her.
Don't let her grow up a fool.
Teach her, thrill her,
Touch her, chill her;
I don't care
If you kill her.
To her mother's "care",
Lewdness, crudeness,
Cruel, demeaning,
Endless violence
Without meaning
Shallow jabs with a knife,
Plenty of pain, lots of blood.
Pleading, screaming,
Enough tears for a flood.
Beatings, kicking her head,
Talking nonstop,

Insulting her, assaulting her
'Til her emotions were dead.
Telling her
So much bunk,
Locking her
In his car trunk.

Then he was at her again,
Pouring out his hate.
All her screams were in vain;
Nobody at church that late.
He took her home

But she got
No sympathy there.
You've school in the morning,
Hurry to bed,
Never noticing
She was half dead.
Oh, by the way,
Will you baptize her?
Men with good records
Those men prefer.

7/17/93

The indications that Vivian A. Hooker not only knew about much of the abuse her daughter was receiving, but seemed to delight in encouraging the abusers, then trying to solve the "mystery" of what had taken place. The student preacher this poem refers to had been a gang leader in a large city in another state before coming to study in the area where much of this story took place. At any age it is improper to be receiving such abuse, but at a month short of thirteen she wasn't the youngest girl this man was abusing. Why none of the adults who had a good idea what was going on did nothing to put a stop to the horror I don't understand. (Dec. 1971)

Son of man, the house of Israel is to me become dross:
all they are brass, and tin, and iron, and lead, in the midst
of the furnace; they are even the dross of silver.

Son of man, say to her, Thou art the land that is not cleansed,
nor rained upon in the day of indignation.

Ezekiel 22: 18 & 24

NO JUSTICE

They're taking wagers
Down there by the lake;
How many customers
Can this girl take?
    He's collecting money;
    She took them all.
    How did my sweetheart
    Into his grip fall?
This isn't the first time,
Nor will it be the last;
Why hasn't he been
Into prison cast?
How dare he treat her
Like she is a toy?
Doesn't it matter
If her life's destroyed?
    Mister, do you like
    What you see going on?
    No, son, I don't at all;
    I'll call the cops on that con.

He knows who's coming,
And he's not dumb;
She's not around
By the time they come.
    Have I lost her forever?
    Who has her now?
    Can her treatment
    Get any worse now?
    Please, Sirs,
    Be careful what you do;
    I want my friend back,
    And I want her alive, too.
She's safely home now,
But I feel depressed.
Why won't they go
And make an arrest?
There is no justice
In this vile land!
Why they don't stop him
I don't understand.

10/24/93 (1972)

    She had tried screaming, fighting, sulking and crying, and other tactics in the past, but nothing worked. All she'd gotten for her efforts was beatings. By this time she'd adopted the coping mechanism of acting silly and egging the guys on. The marijuana they gave her when her fears overcame her loosened her up. They thought she was great fun, and most people thought she was having the time of her life, with no regrets. I knew better. I saw her pain and fears and encouraged her to talk about them. Without that effort to show my concern for her deepest feelings, I'd probably have lost her.

HEBREWS 4: 15?

They gathered around her in the boat
And placed upon her hand a wedding ring,
Laughing and jeering, speaking a sneering note.
What's wrong with you? You'd best enjoy the thing,
'Cause it's the only one you'll ever get;
Nobody will want you when we get done.
So come on; the fun's not over yet.
Come do a favor for each and every one.

Oh God above, with all your might,
Can you understand how a woman feels
When men use her for their delight,
Acting like drunken, disgusting fools?

They gathered around Him in the hall
And placed on his Head a crown of thorns,
Laughing and jeering, one and all.
Away with you, your mother will mourn.
You'll never wear another royal crown.
No one will think you deserve one;
They'll speak your name with a frown.
All for naught will your life have begun.

A crown, a ring, a simple thing.

A taunt, a jeer, a mournful tear.

Another time, another year, new glory does appear—

Now they're not bold, they've no delight, their faces
pale with fright.

A joyous cry, Come home with me, where now are those
who dare disagree?

1/8/94

Since recording this poem I have seen other similar ones. I believe this to be merely a reflection of the theme being an idea whose time has come.

According to their deeds, accordingly he will repay, fury to his adversaries, recompense to his enemies; to the islands he will pay recompense.

So shall they fear the name of the Lord from the west, and his glory from the rising of the sun. When the enemy shall come in like a flood, the Spirit of the Lord shall lift up a standard against him.

Isaiah 59: 18 & 19.

Lewis E. Miles

WIDE EYED

Street names
Mind games
Passions flame
Blow after blow
She doesn't know
She's not dumb
Her mind's numb
Overcome

What's wrong with me,
Am I gonna die?
She looks at me,
Just about to cry.

I'll try to tell you
If what you fear is real
If you will just
Tell me how you feel.

Fat
Especially in the tummy.
All my clothes are tight on me,
And I always gotta pee.

Come on and dry your eyes;
You're not gonna die.

Then you know what's wrong with me?

You're pregnant. You're gonna have a baby.

Really?
Wide eyed and innocent.
How can that be?

Didn't your mother teach you anything?
Anything except how to get in trouble?

Eyes wide. Panic inside.
What do you mean?

I guess we need to talk a while.

OK. Can we find somewhere to sit?

7/19/93

This poem portrays the effects of ignorance and dissociation on an otherwise intelligent fourteen year old. (1973)

BENONI

Some say Hosea
           Of Benoni wrote

But gave away his right
           To what he wrote.

'Twas printed first
           on paper pink, then blue,

Or so say folks
           Who think that is true.

There are others
           Who hold another view—

That there's no proof
           In some supposed clue.

They would simply say,
           "It shows us what league

In which Hosea stands
           With his intrigue."

6/17/99

A COLORFUL STATEMENT

A friend.........Someone asked me to bring this to you.

My response....Why did they think I needed that?

Friend...........You'll know if you look and see.

My response.....I looked, but my mind was blank and flat.

Friend...........Didn't you write the poem on back?

My response.....I guess I did, but I don't understand.
I tried hard to cover my tracks;
Anonymity I'd carefully planned.

Friend...........You did a good job; only a few know,
And we intend to keep the secret well.
We understand it was a crushing blow;
More pain could result if we should tell.

My response.....I'll take it, but in a way it stinks.
No hard feelings intended—
Why did they do it up in pink?
The layout's good, the color should be amended.

Friend...........What color should it be,
Is blue for a boy your choice?
(She spoke thoughtfully,
With sympathy in her voice.)

My response.....Purple, as in a purple heart,
If you want to influence men.
The author was wounded in the heart.
Make it purple if they print it again.

7/18/93

A claim has been heard that the original printing was done with dark pink or red print on pink paper, but that a second printing was done with the same ink on blue paper. The print on the blue paper looked purple, including two little hearts at the top of one section.

WORDS IN THE NIGHT

Wake up, said the angel,
Get up and go get her.
Before my eyes horrors
Flash by like a quick blur.

Lord, I don't understand.
Not that I'll not gladly go;
Did he come at Your command?
That is all I need to know.

I walk down the long hill
With one thing on my mind,
Oblivious to the night chill,
Wondering what I'd find.

Hey you out there,
Come on in.
But I'd no desire
For their din.

Lord, please help me,
I'm shaking from the cold.
Suddenly I feel warm and free,
Ready to make a statement bold.

A guy looks out, white as a sheet.
Who's out on the road with you?
I slowly look up and down the street;
No one is within my view.
Come in or go away!

Lord, you sent me to get the girls out.
You'd do well to do as I say;
Move quickly, don't sit and pout.
I saw what you did to those girls,
And you all ought to be ashamed.
Such evil bars you from gates of pearls;
Repent, or you'll be enflamed!

Some were frightened,
And shook in their shoes.
Another grew bold,
Shouting devilish views.
Don't let him steal our sacrifices.
One's already got away.
We'll just kill that one twice,
And catch the other another day.

I came to rescue one,
But I'll be saving four.
Do you know what I mean,
Or must I tell you more?
Ha ha! He knows!
We got her pregnant for him.
Ain't that guaranteed
To get under his skin!

Now you're talking the fool;
There's not even a chance.
Are you too stoned to know
Why she can't snap her pants?

Cursing, ranting, raving,
Satanic fury spewing forth.
They lost the "perfect sacrifice",
The girl who was the unseen fourth.

What if I'd delayed?
Oh Abby, precious Abigail.
What if I'd not obeyed!
I could not bear to fail.
The joy of the father,
A precious gift of life;
Your grandpa will sign
For my little wife.

Discussion and planning
What we will do.
Said her father,
I've good news for you;
Because of the way you answered
All those in charge at school,
They're not going to kick you out;
They're making an exception to the rule.
Thank you, Lord, You understand.
He already called her my little wife,
Though plots against us her mother planned.
I place in Your hands this gift of life.

Crazy woman, with your knife!
Why'd you cause her such agony
That she feared you'd destroyed her life?
Why'd you have to make promises phony?
She came to my bed in terror
Because of what you'd done.
It's you who is in error,

Paying to kill our daughter and her son.
Fears drive her to run around;
You'll never stop her that way!
In fact, you're loosing ground,
And you crushed our hearts that day.

7/18/93

ANSWERS AND REBUKES

school board rep.... May I ask you
                A few questions?
                To the school board
                I must make suggestions.
                In your defense
                What would you say?
                We're about to meet;
                You must not delay.

my response.........Woe to the inhabitants
                Of this great land.
                Twice woe to those
                Who refuse to understand.
                Woe to the inhabitants
                Of this little valley
                Who behind secrecy
                Continue to rally,
                Who say to the world
                We are people of the Book
                While their abuse is hurled
                Just to let them off the hook.

my charge............Repent—avoid condemnation!
                Tell the truth
                In every situation,
                Even those that seem uncouth.
                Of life's reality
                Receive your portion;
                Don't destroy youth
                By forcing abortion.

board rep............How dare you speak
                To us that way?
                You'll not escape
                Punishment that way!

my response.........How do you know
                I'm not called of the Lord
                Hosea's message
                To bring forward?
                If this thing
                Is of the Lord,
                A little discomfort
                Can you not afford?
                Listen carefully
                And you will see

Proof or denial
Of this reality,
For if the Lord
Has sent me,
They'll stand to object,
But speak to agree.

my lament............Oh, Abigail;
after a pause   Joy of the father,
Why to name you
Did I bother?
For you, my child,
Will die too,
Because this people destroys
Our Father's joy too.

board rep............ So you admit
You'll kill your daughter
And blame others
For the slaughter?

my response.........I am a victim too;
Can't stop the abuse.
To stop that Crazy Woman
I've been of no use.

board rep......... Why did you
Give her another child
When her first *
Drove her mother wild?

my response.........Then said the Lord to me,
Love again a woman
Who is full of adultery,
Though loved by her man—
For they sacrifice
On medicine's high places
All the innocent children
They think are disgraces,
And serve the god
Of worldly education
While shunning
The Lord's Revelation,
For they love snack cakes
More than the truth,
And think nothing of
Condemning hurting youth.

41

a board member... I stood up to speak
to board   Strong words against them
                     But my knees are weak,
                     And I dare not condemn,
                     For an angel
                     Stands before me,
                     Saying, Bless them,
                     Or turn and flee.
                     What good can come
                     I cannot see,
                     But in their favor
                     Let my vote be.

another .... Hosea's message
board   I say he's spoken,
member   And no commandment
                     Has he broken,
                     For her father's long said
                     She's his wife,
                     So we've no right
                     To condemn their life.
                     To a battered girl
                     He has been kind;
                     Can anyone with that
                     Any fault find?

board rep........... We all voted
to me later   To let you stay;
                     From our school
                     You needn't flee away.

my response.........I thought you would,
                     And thank you, sir.
                     I'll keep quiet **
                     If you prefer.

board rep...........Yes, please do.
                     Your point is made,
                     Though a few
                     You'll never persuade.

9/2&3/93

*   Benoni, the child he made reference to, was not her first, just the first one he and most of the members of the community were aware of.

**   This was not the silence of secrecy, of hiding the facts, or of refusing to answer, but rather the quietness that refrains from stirring up trouble for those who did not understand.

And the Pharisees also, who were covetous, heard all these things; and they derided him. And he said unto them, Ye are they which justify yourselves before men; but God knoweth your hearts: for that which is highly esteemed among men is abomination in the sight of God. The law and the prophets were until John: since that time the kingdom of God is preached, and every man presseth into it. And it is easier for heaven and earth to pass, than one tittle of the law to fail. Luke 16: 14-17

And he said unto him, If they hear not Moses and the prophets, neither will they be persuaded, Though one rose from the dead. Luke 16: 31

COMING AND GOING

her request...... Will you go with me
To church homecoming?
my answer...... I'll think about it;
That's not my kind of thing.
my prayer.......Lord, show me what to do.
the answer......Dreams of horror that night.
my answer......Yes, I'll accompany you;
to her   I understand your fright.

her lament........I wish we didn't have to go.
Sabbath AM   I'd rather go elsewhere with you,
But my mother carries on so,
I don't know what else to do.
my advice....... Stay close to me as much as you can;
Try to avoid that preacher man.
For your protection God has a plan;
I'll carry it out if I can.

preacher man....Let me have her once more
after lunch   For old times sake.
my answer...... Not on your life,
You sneaky snake.
It is no wonder you
Got run out of New York.
You're earning no respect
Acting like a dork.

later..............Come on, dad,
It's time to go;
We've seen enough
Of that gangster's show.

Sun AM.........Hello Samson.
my response... Hello, Dreamboat,
Why'd ya call me that?
That's a strange note.
Dreamboat's...'Cause you're the
answer   Strongest man I've met;
No one else ever
Stood up to him yet.

| biker…………..Heard you ran |
a few days	Big Richard out of town.
later	Now if that don't turn
	The world upside down!
My reply………Thanks for the compliment;
	God is great.
	People His power
	Underestimate.

7/20/93

Preacher Man was unmasked. "Dreamboat" was his gang queen. I called her that to let her know that I realized she wasn't a monster like he was, but simply couldn't escape his control.

THE PHOTOGRAPHER

School pictures.

Not so cool pictures.

Against the rules pictures.

Is this the Positive Way?

Those actions straight from Hell—

You pray they'll turn out well?!?

Can't you see, Bible teacher man,

The evil of your perverted plans?

I will stop you if I can.

9/30/93

How many students did he abuse in
this manner? Perhaps nobody knows
the answer to that question, but
the activities went on during more
than one school year, mainly because
people were loath to believe there
was any reason to investigate the rumors.

All too often, much evil which could have been checked is allowed to take place with Little or no protest or intervention. Adherence to the principles outlined in the Christian Bible in regard to finding out whether things are true, and as is needed, administering Reproof to the erring ones is neglected, and much needless suffering takes place.

NO ESCAPE

Reality's contortion;
Abortion after forced abortion.
Try to stop it,
Still her portion.
Hateful, abusive mother.
One abuser, then another;
Now an unknown
Older brother.
Lying, denying mother,
Think the truth you can smother?

unknown.........Let me have her,
brother (To use her for things
        No man had oughter)
        You can have my daughter.
my reply.........No. I promised her father
        I'd stay with her for life;
        To ask again you needn't bother,
        Unless you want to stir up strife.
unknown.........Then take them both.
brother   Let them support you.
My reply.........No, 'twould violate my oath,
        And I don't wish to learn from you.
        I'll not stoop to be a pimp
        Nor fall for your trap;
        With sharp words I'll not skimp
        If you don't shut your trap.

My words......I know it is hard,
To her   But you need to do your work.
        They're gonna help me
        Protect you from that jerk.

7/22/93

We were working at a summer camp when this man who claimed to be her oldest brother got her pregnant. Her mother tried to give her to this man, who she denied being related to at all.

He had also gotten his wife's oldest daughter pregnant, then tried to blame me. His goal seemed to be control of my wife so he could prostitute her. She was so humiliated and devastated by the combined results of his abuse, her mother's, and the condemnation of those who should have been sympathetic and supportive, that she couldn't function to fulfill her job of doing the camp laundry.

I was relieved of part of my responsibilities so I could sit with her, encourage her, and help her get her work done. (1976)

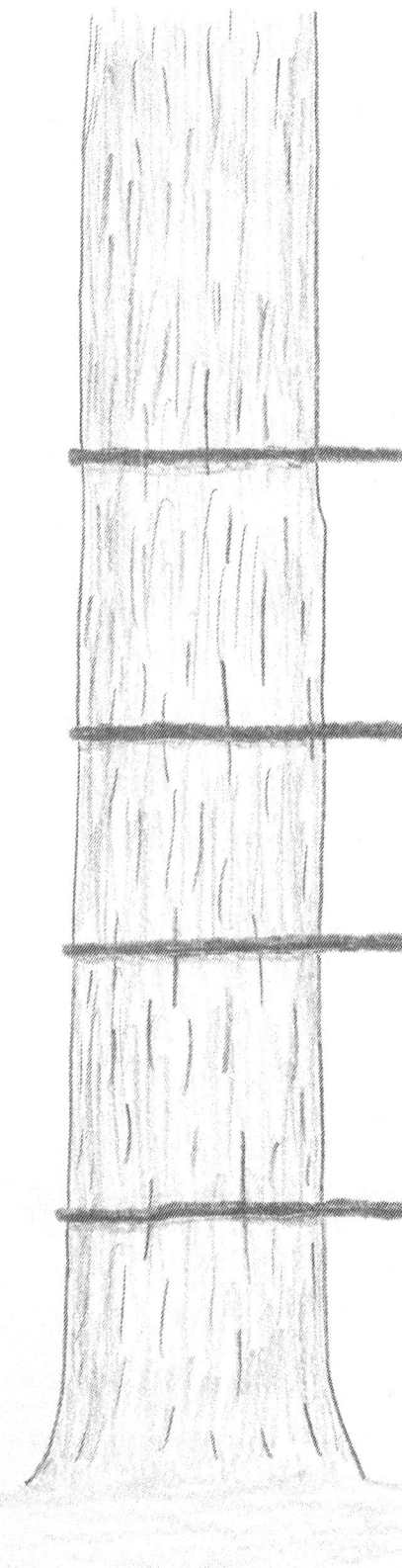

"CRUCIFY HER"

At Reflection Riding
tied to a tree,
Cold and naked
for all to see;
Cold and thirsty,
needing a drink;
Fear and cold driving
her to the brink.
She'd been there all night,
since before dark—
When would people start
riding through the park?

Hallucinations—her tormentors
are coming back.
They're staring at her—
dare she look back?
She sees a stranger who
says he'll return.
A glimpse of her boyfriend;
how her heart yearns.

Coffee and Cornflakes are
all they have;
No medications except
stinky horse salve.
She doesn't care as long
as it is warm.

Who has done this
atrocity to you?
To tell on them she
fears to do.
"I don't know who
those guys were."
(Though one was closely
related to her.)

Who masterminded this
Disgusting scene?
Who could be so
incredibly mean?
None but a cruel
older brother,
And a demented,
crazy mother.

3/12/94

STILL A CHILD

Just sign your name
On this line.
You needn't be ashamed;
All will be fine.

Words of hope
Ring in her mind,
But no courage
Could she find.
"You're eighteen now;
You don't need consent
To make a vow.
Let her resent, RESENT, RESENT!
Say no to her. No, NO, NO!
Come be my bride.
She'd concur,
But she's too weak inside.
She signs.

What happened?
I thought we agreed—
No more abortions
We'd concede.

I'm sorry.
It was awful.
She made me sign
To make it lawful.

7/22/93

What kind of threats her mother held over her if she didn't obey her is something I do not know. Because of the extreme abusive control having been exercised over her for such a long time, she was so easily frightened that it wouldn't have taken much. Her mother solicited the nurses help and sympathy by claiming her daughter had been attacked and raped, and that she didn't even have a boyfriend who was interested in marrying her, and that she had been a virgin before the attack. None of those claims were true, at least not in the sense her mother intimated, but the woman could be convincing. The power of her mother's complete control over her was not reduced until a few months later when we talked with the preacher who we were asking to perform a church wedding for us. We told him she was pregnant <u>before</u> we told her parents. Breaking the "secrecy" began the long, slow process of breaking her mother's stranglehold of control over her. (1977)

TURNING POINT

How dare they let her
Parade up the aisle
In a white dress?
Don't they see
Her life is a mess?

We see, said friends,
How much she needs,
How much her future depends,
On our encouragement;
A crowd of friends,
Some burning tapers,
A ceremony, a party,
That special piece of paper.

They came,
Signed their names,
Gave their presents,
Most of all, their presence.

7/18/93

At the reception following the ceremony, someone who knew something about how much time had passed since her father had first called her my wife the first time cracked a joke about what was happening. That wasn't really a wedding, he said. It was a political statement. In a very real sense he was right. We had chosen the fifth anniversary of the date on which the Supreme Court of the United States of America ruled in favor of abortion on demand. It was all at once a protest, a defense of our son's right to life, and as my bride would later state, her emancipation proclamation, freeing her from slavery to her mother's every whim.

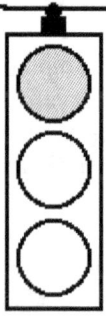

THE LORD OF LIGHTNING

A Satanic sign
    Is their design
        To keep Hosea out. *
They think he'll pine
    On the sideline
        While they raise devilish shouts

A Satanic sign
    Is his design
        To let the truth ring out.
        He gives the sign
            And with pantomime
                The conflict he spells out. **

Hosea, to his wife.........Oh, there you are
        What's in the jar
        You're about to drink?
her reply...........................It is a mystery—
        They mixed it up for me.
           Taste and see what you think.

Hosea's observation......That sure is nasty stuff
        They surely treat you rough;
           'Tis an abortion drink. ***
        The evil hearted men
           Who enter Satan's den—
            From nothing will they shrink!

Hosea's statement of faith...No sacrifice tonight;
        The Lord will guide our flight,
        And this wee one will live.

A cult member...............That guard has failed his job—
        The low down filthy slob.
        This prophet must not live.
        I'll stab him in the back
           And he will not come back;
                I'll make him like a sieve.
           I have him in my hand,
           And we'll proceed as plann'd!
        His child must never live.

Hosea reacts...............Hosea lifts his hand.
        Lord, please stretch forth your hand
        And open scaly eyes.

the answer.................A brilliant flash of light
    Illuminates the night
     From out of starry skies.

a cultist.....................Hail now, Great Lord of Luck—
    That horrid prophet's struck!
     'Twill be a great demise!

another cultist............O splendid heap of dung,
    Your time has just been sprung,
     And I sure think it nice!

    Hosea still stands,
     For he's in the Lord's hands,
      And his job is not done yet.
       From a death with no grave
        His child will yet be saved
         Despite the evil threat.
        Like a great condenser
       Of fire from God's censer,
      Hosea's glowing yet.
     The charge leaps to the knife,
    Which, raised to take his life,
   Its mission will forget.

Hosea, to bystanders...Help him, for he is hurt.
    Fear not, he is inert.
     Of all electric charge.

examiner ....His heart is awful still,
    And his breathing is nill;
     The chance he's dead is large.

Hosea's prayer.........Our Father, Lord of Love,
    Send new life from above—
     Forgive his evil charge.

Hosea's instructions...Please help him to his feet.
    God's gift of life is sweet,
     And His power is large.

      12/27/95

---

* The pass code to get past the guards
** Hosea claimed not to know American Sign Language,

but someone claimed he signed Isaiah 14: 12—20
*** A potion to induce premature labor, to provide a sacrifice.

Through fraud, coercion, and blackmail, and through the temptations of idle curiosity and power seeking, a number of Christians had been drawn into the group which was practicing ritual abuse and Satanism. Their Lord had heard their united prayers asking for a sign of assurance that they had not gone too far, that they could escape the power of the group, and that He was still with them.

While I knew there were those who did not wish to be involved, I did not know about their united prayers. I knew only that an angel had brought me a message of promised deliverance for our son. Upon arrival I gave the sign of the goat with my fingers crossed behind my back, signifying that I did <u>not</u> believe in their ceremonies, but my bluff was called. I would have to do more than that to get past the guards without swearing allegiance to Satan. Time for prayer—Lord God of creation, Ruler of all the unfallen worlds, You sent me here to rescue my son, but I can't get past the guards. What shall I do? As an answer,

the blessing of the Holy Spirit came over me, moving me to "speak" in a "tongue" I did not know, American Sign Language, to portray the passage from Isaiah mentioned in the footnote.

The next miracle came when someone tried to distract and frighten me by showing me a gun collection laid out in a van parked there. Thinking only about the destruction of the earth at the end of time, I lamented that it was a shame that such beautiful artwork as what was etched and carved on the weapons would soon perish. I was thinking that such talent could surely have been put to something of more eternal worth than decorating guns. What I didn't know was that everything I touched in that collection would be miraculously destroyed that night. Stainless steel would become a crumbled, brittle substance which sloughed off powdery residue. A beautifully carved cypress stock rotted, and other unheard of things happened.

After examining the gun collection and pronouncing the lament, I excused myself and proceeded past the other guard lines into the ritual area, where I found my wife about to drink a substance her mother was insisting she needed. I tasted it, then poured it out on the ground so she couldn't be forced to drink it. At that point the knife wielder decided to take action.

Not only did God provide a bolt out of a star filled sky, He worked more wonders. I was unharmed. My attacker, although revived, was hospitalized. For three days he couldn't let go of that knife, nor could it be pried out of his hand. Not until he sent word asking that I pray that he be able to release it did he succeed in letting go of it.

In the moments after the lightning incident, someone noticed that not only did I seem to glow, but when I walked past a car, the headlights lit up. A 110 volt light bulb gave light even when taken out of the socket. I stated that this was to show that God is the true source of power and light. Someone angrily smashed the light bulb on the hood of a car. Instead of putting out the light, that precipitated something even stranger. Fireworks erupted from the fragments, and when they subsided, every fragment of the shattered bulb glowed, giving off more light than when it was intact.

Before my wife and I left, we turned over the table and the altar. We washed our hands and quenched our thirst with the ordinary distilled water they had proclaimed as holy water, then poured the rest out on the ground as a thank offering to the God of our salvation.

The prayers of the believers who united in asking for a sign of deliverance had been answered, not once, not twice, but in abundance. The cult members tried to discredit the witnesses, and to cover up evidence, but someone who had been present dug up the buried weapons and showed them to others. For three days the unreleasable knife gave testimony to the power of God, and even the cult members angry accusations gave testimony that their magic was no match for the power of the God of Creation.

LITTLE DETAILS

Hey; we respect you just the same,

But didn't you choose the wrong name?

With Athaliah you did clash;

Shouldn't his name be Joash? *

I hid him in the house of praise,

A little less trouble to raise;

I really did use that name—

At least the letters are the same.

Oh no, they most certainly are not!

One letter quite diff'rent you've got. **

So you like my "h" with the hidden tail,

Making you guess how I did prevail?

God is the healer of broken-ness.

The name, Jason, does confess

That His deliverance is no tall tale,

So why quibble over a letter's tail?

1/31/94

* See II Chronicles 22: 10—12.

** Compare the letters of Jason with
those of Joash, and notice how close to
identical the two sets of letters are—
only the height of the "tail" of the
last letters is different.

THE BATTLE BELONGS TO THE LORD

revelers ....What are you doing here!?
　　　　　　　　Should you not shake with fear?

Hosea ....At God's command I'll go
　　　　　　　　Wherever He does show,
　　　　　　　　For He has promised me
　　　　　　　　Protection certainly.

revelers ....Well, you believed a lie;
　　　　　　　　It is your night to die.

Hosea ....Surely as He sent me,
　　　　　　　　You cannot murder me.

a reveler.............O block of densest wood,
　　　　　　　　Your head I'm splitting good.
　　　　　　　　You'll fuel our fire tonight,
　　　　　　　　To everyone's delight.

the results............A super splitting maul,
　　　　　　　　Inertial splitting pawl,
　　　　　　　　(A wood chopper's delight)
　　　　　　　　Against an angel's might
　　　　　　　　Is naught, and so was it—
　　　　　　　　To use no longer fit.

another reveler......He will not be so hot
　　　　　　　　If with this gun he's shot;
　　　　　　　　'Twill punch his magic shield,
　　　　　　　　And the ghost he will yield.

the results..........Hole in front, hole in back,
　　　　　　　　Bullet through shirt did hack.
　　　　　　　　Although wearing the shirt,
　　　　　　　　Hosea is not hurt.

a third reveler......This spring launched, flying knife
　　　　　　　　Will surely end his life,
　　　　　　　　Then we can have his wife
　　　　　　　　Without all this strife.
　　　　　　　　He sets the launcher's spring,
　　　　　　　　Then checks everything.
　　　　　　　　He lets the sharp blade fly
　　　　　　　　With a loud, gleeful cry.

reaction ....I cannot understand.
    He lifted up his hand
    The flying blade to catch,
    And got narry a scratch!

another reaction....Something is awfully wrong;
    How can one ring the gong *
    When hearing his swan song,
    His own life to prolong?

Hosea...............God is good, God is strong;
    'Tis He who rings the gong
    To save one from life's song. **
    Worship Him and be strong!

Hosea, to his wife..Let's go home, precious one.
    Our daughter's time's not done,
    For God's the Gracious One
    Who saved her and our son.
    His name alone be prais'd,
    For He our hope has rais'd
    His name alone be prais'd!

12/27/95

---

* This comment refers to The Gong Show, a program in which amateur performers were put on stage for an audition. Failing, substandard, or otherwise unsatisfactory performances were halted by the ringing of a gong.

** For the wages of sin is death, but the gift of God is eternal life through Jesus Christ our Lord
Romans 6: 23

---

* *

The cultists were angered by the escape of some of their subjects from their power, and enraged over the embarrassment they had suffered when some of their claims were proven to be false. Some who also wished to leave the cult, but had not managed to make a clean break became their target. They set them up for failures, then taunted them that they weren't going to escape because they didn't have enough faith, and that they couldn't be forgiven because they had gone too far and had been too bad for God to want them. The cultists wanted to extinguish any hope they had of ever separating themselves from the cult. Time had passed, and in some cases the cultists had nearly succeeded. At a time when some of these victims of the cruel system had nearly reached a state of complete hopelessness, the Lord again used Hosea to provide another sign of assurance of deliverance and hope.

FOR BETTER OR FOR WORSE

a friend..........You'd best come with me to town;
          Your wife is running all around.
my response....Why do you show such dismay?
          I said she could have the truck today.
friend ....You don't understand what I mean;
          She's down there making a regular scene.
          She's walking up and down the street
          Accosting every well dressed man she meets.

my thoughts....I wonder what triggered off her fears.
          Will she do this for all her years?
my request......Come with me, let's go back to camp.
          That's enough acting like a tramp.
her answer......I don't have to listen to you.
          Or let you tell me what to do.
my retort.........My house has wheels, you know;
          I can move on if you act so.
her response....See there, I knew you'd treat me mean!
          All you want is to make a scene.

my question....What are you doing under my hood?
my friends......To run for her I didn't think it should,
response   So I pulled loose some wires,
          Fixing it so it wouldn't fire,
          After I moved it under this tree.
          Our baby sitting service this time is free.
my reply........ Thanks, please take them on with you;
          I don't know how much I have to do.

to a stranger.... Where is she now, have you seen her, sir?
stranger .... You've a lot of nerve to admit being connected to her.
my reply........ Yes, I'm connected to my poor confused wife.
          If I can calm her she'll cease this strife.
stranger .... She's down at the police station, making a scene.
          They're looking for you, if you know what I mean.

officer .... Who are you, and what do you want?
          Why'd you choose our town to haunt?
my reply........ I'm sorry my wife has made such a scene,
          But she's not after wads of green.
          She was treated terrible as a child;
          Sometimes her fears drive her wild.
          May I please talk with her?
          Perhaps some other memory I can stir.
another cop..... Hurry up, there she goes;
          Trying to stop the wind when it blows?

<pre>
my plea..........Sound of music, sound of pain.
                 Don't want to hear that again.
                 Please hush, that's making it worse—
                 It reminds her of her mother's curse.

my entreaty......Hey, come back here!
                 Please, Wiggle Butt. *
                 Who pushed you off
                 In that old rut?

her response......I've got to go now;
                 It's been nice to see ya.
                 By the way,
                 My name's Maria.
my entreaty......OK, Maria.
                 Come home with me;
                 I'll always love you,
                 Whatever your name might be.
her reply.........I need to go to the store—
                 Don't be a dope.
my question.....What for?
her answer...... To get a bar of soap. **
my statement... I want you to come with me back to camp
                 And quit running around like a tramp.
her rebuttal...... No. You can't want me now.
my answer...... Yes. For better or worse was my vow.
</pre>

7/24 & 29/93

* Wiggle Butt was an affectionate nickname that was connected to some of her pleasant memories. It had been the result of what I had hoped would be a private joke, but she laughed and went to tell her friends what I had called her. Maria, on the other hand, was a name her mother and some of her other abusers called her when setting her up for abuse.

** A bar of soap was a reference both to an imaginary childhood friend and to one of her dissociative identities. If I accused her of disturbing my work equipment or personal belongings, she would sometimes giggle and tell me she didn't do it—a bar of soap did.

She came back to my house on wheels, which we lived in because of the line of work I was engaged in at the time, contract forestry, primarily hand planting pine seedlings. What had set her off? Some old foes had settled in that town, and had wasted no time in trying to take full advantage. They had probably told her I wouldn't want her back.

They, of course, couldn't have cared less what I wanted, or what she really wanted.

AND FOR MUCH WORSE

Stress of life like so much wine.
Crossing the threshold of consciousness,
Unable to see through her design
For getting us each in a mess.
  She's down the road again, acting wild.
  She's no thought for anything,
  Not even the care of her own child,
  Thinking only of her self-hateful fling.
Wake up, Hosea, from your bad dream
Of strange women in bed with you.
Like a dream did reality seem;
No power to stop the view.
     Hey! What are you doing here?
    Leave me alone, both of you.
   Your sweetheart sent us here.
   No, I want nothing from you.
    Oh, do you think you're better than us?
   No, but why'd you do this to me?
   Why do you make such a fuss;
   Are you afraid good times to see?
No, you made me violate my vow.
To never pull that stunt again
You both must promise me now,
For it can only cause us pain.
What will your husband say
When he learns what you have done?
To him surely nothing you'll say!
I'll not hide the truth from anyone.
  Oh, maybe it's good you stopped us;
  Someone is looking for you.
  We about got caught in your bus,
  And that surely wouldn't do.
You better come get your wife,
Or if not, at least your children.
I've not seen such wildness in my life;
I find it totally bewilderin'.

later.......What kind of man are you
   To allow such things to go on?

  I hadn't the slightest clue;
  Such things I frown upon.
  If I could stop her I surely would,
  But doing that is beyond me.
  If I could calm her I would,
  But her motivation is a mystery.

Oh, my children, my children,
How much did they see
That was frightening and bewilderin'?
Oh, the thought brings misery!

8/2/93

WHO CAN KNOW?

Who can know Hosea's song?
Who can know if he ever did wrong?
Did he ever make a mistake
As to which prostitute to take?
Was he always true to his wife,
Or did he too lead a double life?
These details of fact we're not told,
So before we make a statement bold,
Let us ask ourselves why we care
Whether he wandered here and there,
Or traveled as straight as an arrow true,
Never loosing focus or point of view.
Do we seek our own sins to excuse,
And to admit the truth seek to refuse?
Or are we not sure God will be fair
If He sees fit the untrue to spare?
Don't ask Hosea whether he is sure
If his life has always been pure,
For if he's truthful he'll surely say,
"I need the Savior day by day."

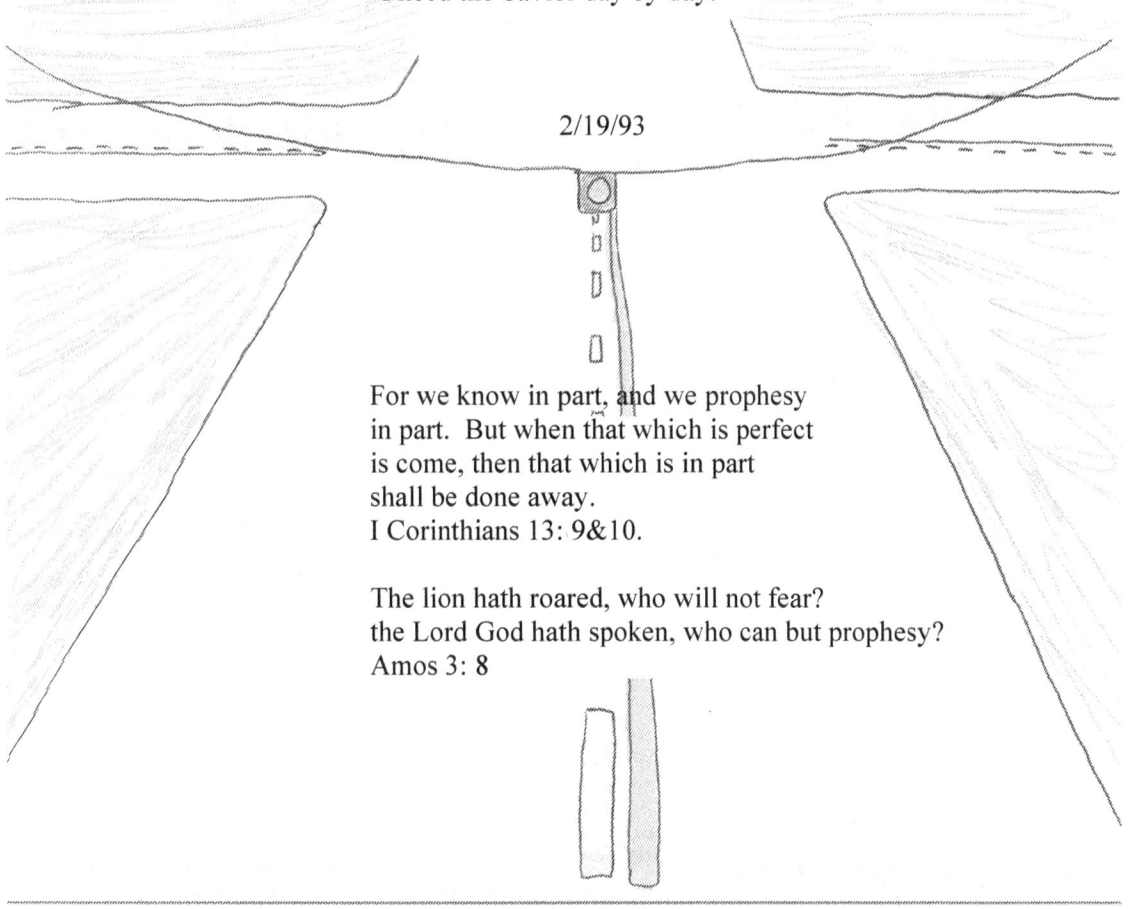

2/19/93

For we know in part, and we prophesy
in part. But when that which is perfect
is come, then that which is in part
shall be done away.
I Corinthians 13: 9&10.

The lion hath roared, who will not fear?
the Lord God hath spoken, who can but prophesy?
Amos 3: 8

A JOKE OR A THREAT?

a friend............	Hosea, Dr. K's in town.
my reply.........	Am I supposed to be impressed?
friend	You better batten your hatches down,
	Or you might be distressed.
my reply..........	I already knew, but thanks for the hint.
	As far as how much he influences me,
	I brush him off like so much lint.
	By the way, what's he doing in Tennessee?
friend	You're asking me—I thought you knew!
my response......	I wouldn't have to know, I could guess,
	And we probably have about the same view,
	But I'd like to hear your opinion expressed.
friend's view.....	He wants more workers for the cereal factory;
	I think you know what that means.
my reply..........	Yes, I don't find Cornflakes satisfactory.
	I'm allergic to corn, if you know what I mean.
	They already tried to kidnap her once,
	Although she doesn't know.
	They must think I'm a dunce,
	Or they'd know I'd never go.
to the police......	Sirs, these men are up to no good;
	They're stockpiling weapons and strife.
	You'd do well to stop them if you could;
	At least once they tried to kidnap my wife.
officers	We agree with you, and we wish we could.
	We're inclined to believe your report is true.
	If we had hard evidence we would,
	But as it is, we can't help you.
my warning......	Watch out, Cornflake,
	Or you might get burned twice.*
	This time you ought to listen
	To your father's advice.
to a friend........	Double dealing, forked tongued,
	False Christ, Son of a Devil;
	About his grand intentions
	Can't they see there's nothing level?
Cornflake, ...	You're a hard one to keep track of;
some time later	What are you doing in South Carolina?
	We've got a job in mind we think you'd love;
	For it we can't think of anyone finer.
my response.....	You and your craze
	For Bible names.

All you want is my wife.
I see through your games.
If you manage to take her,
The name Rahab will she bear.
Heavenly protection will go with her;
A scarlet cord would hang for her there.

after a pause….. Tell your friend I called him
Joseph Smith the Thirteenth,
And that Jericho will fall again;
There'll be a fiery reward for him.**

7/19/93

* David Koresh, long before he had legally
       changed his name from Vernon Howell,
       joked openly about burning his compound,
       and how he planned to build it to make sure
       the job would be easy to do. I tried to get
       others to take this as a real threat.
** That was my last warning to Cornflake.

Several years of sporadic but intense confrontations with these characters took place
at different locations across the southeastern states took place. Some even joked about
my having run Big Richard out of town, but that I didn't even make Vernon Howell. The
next poem is about what turned out to be one last showdown, moments after my comment
about Joseph the Thirteenth and Jericho.

UNSEEN WARRIOR

They wave a pistol as they start to pass,
Then, with a startled look, let off the gas.
They try again, and again chicken out.
I can't hear them, but I see them shout.
Whatever their fear, it must be a doozie,
'Cause now they wave the pistol and an Uzi.

on CB............   Why are you looking at me?
                    I don't understand.
trucker .... It's not you I'm looking at;
                    Where's the other man?
my reply.........   There's no one with me,
                    Is that not plain?
                    He must have been an angel,
                    That's all I can explain;
                    I didn't see him.
trucker .... Well, he was a sight!
                    Loaded with weapons,
                    All shining and bright.

8/26/93

How often angels intervene to protect us we don't know, but since the devil would like to be rid of all interference to his evil plot, perhaps we only see isolated incidents in an ongoing struggle. Another driver claimed that after they turned around, they stopped to battle an unbelievably bright red rope which wriggled back into their car as fast as they tried to throw it out. The "rope" then disappeared.

REPROBATE MINDS

stranger ....Hey man, look at this;
Ain't that a picture of bliss?

my reply.........Those pictures have been around;
Ain't ya coverin' any new ground?

stranger ....Sure, man, come see what I've got—
They're young, fresh, and hot.
Come over, and bring a friend.
On a good time you can depend.

my response.....Hey officer, be my friend.
Give him some time to spend.

news ....Self proclaimed Porn King arrested
When an unidentified man protested.

my thoughts......I cry for you, Maria.
about   How many men got to see ya?
related   No hiding and no escape
events   From men desiring to rape,
                 Saying, "I know you, you're Maria.
                 It's about time I got to feel ya."

8/17/93

The pictures of objection were taken at school by one of the teachers, but they were no school pictures. When this teacher was about to get caught, he sold everything in his collection of contraband pictures for something like fifty dollars, just to get rid of evidence. He had his own darkroom in his office, which he also used for proper school photography, but kept the other ones locked in a file cabinet hidden behind the regular ones. The purchaser was from out of state, but that didn't help "Maria" when she and her husband moved. The little "biography" which was published with pictures of her stated that she thought she was thirteen, and acted like she was. It also claimed she liked a number of disgusting activities which she has assured her closest friends were not voluntary, and that the torment haunted her for many years.

HOSEA'S DUEL

Hosea ....   It's story time
And with my rhyme
With your mind I'll play
They think I'll scream
'Cause they stole my cream,
But they can't touch my curds and whey.

rival ....   No conceit,
But you admit defeat,
Even if you don't scream,
Because much better is the cream.

Hosea............   The cream's the part
That destroys men's hearts,
Then they haul corpses away.
I'll eat the curds,
Throw skimmers to the birds
And beasts looking for prey.

Rival ....   Well, when we get down to words that
sting,
I could say many terrible things.

Hosea.........   If you can make it terrible,
I can make it worse.
If you can say it forward,
I can say it in reverse.

rival ....   Your tongue will surely tangle;
I'll beat you from some angle.

Hosea ....   I'll teach you about angle
And how the fish get tangled.
Come close, you foolish fish;
Come nibble if you wish,
But you'd best stop with a look,
'Cause I'm just waitin' to set the hook.

Rival..........   I'll be the one to laugh.
You'll be left with half.
I'll empty your worm can;
You've not such a perfect plan.

Hosea........   I can dig worms by the river,
I can dig worms by the lakes,

I can dig them in the desert,
And I'll do whatever it takes.
Don't think you'll steal all my worms—
You'll be the one that squirms,
Because I have a plan
That'll have you in the frying plan.*

rival ....   I thought I heard you repeat
That you had given up eating meat.

Hosea...........   I remember the taste,
I remember the smell.
And still I sometimes slobber,
For I liked it well.
Don't taunt me at my table
Unless you want to cry.
Laugh if you are able,
But only if you're ready to fry.**

2/23/93

* This was a statement about consequences, which I was willing to
see that he faced, and not meant as a threat other than that.

** A reference to hell.

An unwelcome "guest" had inserted himself into Hosea's household so he could
Have access to Hosea's wife. His wife did not welcome him either, but was too
frightened to say she didn't want him around, or to tell Hosea what the bully was forcing
her to endure.

This unwelcome person tried hard to come up with ways to make Hosea look like an
unreasonable, inhospitable person. One day, trying to cover up how seriously he really
meant his challenge, he jeered at Hosea, who by this time had caught on and said that in
no way was the guy welcome, what would you do if I challenged you to a duel?

Hosea thought a moment, and, realizing that he dare not show a reaction which could
be interpreted as cowardice or insecurity if he was to make progress toward getting this
foe to leave, said that he'd probably take him up on the challenge. This said, Hosea
asked him, you are aware, aren't you, that the person being challenged gets to choose the
weapons? An answer to the affirmative came back. Well, in that case, Hosea stated, I
choose as my weapon my tongue; I think I could lick you with it. (pun intended) That
choice and the confidence he had were not based on a belief of superiority, for it was
known that this individual could outdo him when it came to tongue twisters.

Hosea's confidence was based on the fact that three things were in his favor: the laws
of the land in which he resided, social expectations and pressures, and a clarity of
conscience which his adversary couldn't possibly have.

DESPAIR AND COURAGE

Hosea's predicament.......Plotting, scheming, unwelcome guest,
Sneering, laughing at my request
That he leave and not return,
Saying that he deserves his turn.
Says he to me, "I had her first."
Your fortune should now be reversed.

Plotting, scheming, double binding,
His own business seldom minding.

Hosea's prayer............Lord, chase away our live in foe.

the answer................For now, says He, the answer's no.

the foe's trouble....................The cult man now is suspect
In a dismal murder case.
Hosea will not help him
A sound alibi to place.

the foe's response...........................You'll pay for this, you traitor;
Just how you'll find out later.

He took her in the market
He raped her by the square.
He forced her in her own house
When Hosea wasn't there.

the Lord's intervention........................... A miracle of timing—
She now bears Hosea's child,
Though oppressed by her cult man,
And so many times defiled.

Hosea's reaction...........................Hosea's hot with anger
Against her mean, longtime foe,
But thankful for the new gift
Of life God did bestow.

Gomer's weakness....................No strength to tell Hosea,
No strength to call police,
No strength to tell her cult man
To go with him she will cease,
But miracle of miracles,
She's gathered strength to stay
The efforts of her cult man
To take her child to slay.

the foe flees............................Although he's not arrested,
                              No longer does he stay,
                              With odds now stacked against him,
                              And Hosea boiling so.
                              He knows that he is loosing,
                              And that it is time to go.

Hosea's prayers of thanks..........Oh give thanks unto the Lord,
                              For with patience He has scored
                              Salvation for a wee life.
                              Though born midst scenes of vile strife,
                              He has brought contentment
                              To me and my precious wife.

                              Oh give thanks forever more;
                              A new victory did He score,
                              For she now has strength to say,
                              I will choose Hosea's way.

12/30/95

By faith Enoch was translated that he should not see death; and was not found, because God translated him: for before his translation he had this testimony, that he pleased God. Hebrews 11: 5

Verily I say unto you, Among them that are born of women there hath not risen a greater than John the Baptist ~ ~ ~ for all the prophets and the law prophesied unto John. And if you will receive it, this is Elias which is to come. From Matthew 11: 11—14

Can any believer dispute that Enoch and John the Baptist were both men of faith who pleased God? One walked right into Heaven, while the other languished in prison until he was executed. Great faith and miraculous deliverance do not always coincide.

Some of the most faithful have been tempted with discouragement. Even Jesus cried out, My God, my God, why hast Thou forsaken me? Since we are told He knew no sin, and lived and died a perfect life, this expression of anguish cannot be considered sinful. Let us be merciful to ourselves and to those around us, and not pass evil judgement on the motives behind cries of distress.

Whether called to show great signs of God's power, or to the agony of helping show the true nature of evil, we can know that God will not forget us, and that in the end He will reward us for our faithfulness.

WALTER'S BLESSING

The builder gets the inheritance,

Computer man will be the priest,

But you will be the prophet;

Begin when I'm deceased

To reveal the family secrets—

God's kingdom will be increased.

Spoken December 1989
Recorded 3/22/93 in this format.

This was Walter's response to a discussion about the blessings given by the patriarchs of the Bible.

When he first spoke something similar, he used names. I challenged him to say the same thing without using any names. After a bit he spoke this version.

What is a prophet? Is he/she some exalted, holy person of some special merit? No. I Corinthians chapter twelve shows that prophecy is one of the gifts of the Spirit, all of which God gives as he pleases.

I Samuel 9:9 says, "(Beforetime in Israel, when a man went to enquire of God, thus he spake, Come and let us go to the seer: for *he that is* now *called* a Prophet was beforetime called a Seer.)" A prophet, then,

Is a seer; one who sees—one who is not blind. Revelation 3:18 says, "I counsel thee ~ ~ ~ anoint thine eyes with eyesalve, that thou mayest see."

A TIMELY VISIT

A kind looking man came to visit
One Sabbath day at our church,
And I asked myself, "What is it
That caused my heart to lurch
When I heard his name
And saw his kind face."
I thought it was a shame
That no memory could I place.

When he talked of attending GC * Session,
And how he was from Bass Lake,
Memory still eluded my possession,
Though I did a second double take.

Then all of a sudden I knew;
He used to be a Colporteur, **
And the memories flew,
And began to fall in order.
Why sure, I know about that man;
He had sold grandpa that good book
That talked about salvation's plan
And led the family to the beliefs they took.

Later I asked him, You're from Bass Lake?
Well, my people are from there too.
Does the name Thompson any memory make?
Yes, I knew Ernie, and Fred and Nellie too.
I'm Fred and Nellie's grandson,
And you sold grandpa that book.
Let me guess—you're the son of which one?
And to enjoy guessing he partook.
Let's see, perhaps you are Jim's,
Or maybe Katie's first up.
No, I'm Mickey's, not Kate or Jim's'
I'm the kid who wouldn't shut up.
And you're active in the church?
That gives me good reason to smile,
And gives my old heart an encouraging lurch;
I'm as happy as I've been for a while.

His smile faded to a frown
I don't see how you survived—
Who helped you deal with that clown?
Surely some help you derived!

Yes, I knew about his Chicago "Bosses",
And the unflavored gelatin bag, ***
Much about the double crosses,
And why Tom's life did sag.
I knew the devil walked
In the tracks of a roaring Lion;
He tried when people walked
To keep them from reaching New Zion.
Who protected me from the provoker?
I had help from a Roarin' Lion,
A Mad Dog, a Joker,****
And the Ruler of Mt. Zion.

He said, I've new joy in my heart.
To come down here
And see you doing your part!
I'm glad you persevered.

Little could he know
The sadness of my heart;
Of courage run so low
It needed his jumpstart,
For I was 'bout crushed with grief
And to share with anyone not dared.
Though his visit was brief,
It reminded me that people cared.

12/4/93

*General Conference
**A salesman of religious books and periodicals
***that particular bag contained hard drugs, not gelatin
****aliases which he may or may not have remembered.

FLASHBACK

My soul, it is weary;
Yes, and my heart is sore.
I think I'm done grieving,
Then I remember more.

His hand grips my finger,
But it tugs at my heart;
Why was it they took him
'Fore I could do my part
To wrap his wee fingers
'Round his grandmother's heart?

They said they'd bring him back—
Their words I know were true,
For they did not know what
That crazy one would do.

His grandma went crazy,
And I do not know why
She was so determined
That Benoni should die—
Stole him from the nurs'ry,
And no one saw her go.
She hid him by the pumps
That make the suction go.
So they wouldn't heear him
Should someone venture by,
She taped his sweet mouth shut
To make sure he'd not cry.

He survived four more hours,
And he was still alive,
But he was so weakened
That he did not survive.

They didn't let me hold him,
Or even tell me why,
When they could not find him,
Although they surely tried.
All that they could answer
Was just to nod and cry.

6/1/93

Sometimes grief or shock can be so intense that the person experiencing the emotional reaction cannot fully handle the load. Part of the emotional load, or perhaps even the memory of the events is pushed into the recesses of the mind and not retrieved until strength is gained to deal with the stress.

When what is stored is finally retrieved it may come out unexpectedly, flashing at the person nearly as intensely as if they were re-experiencing the traumatic event.

THE PROPOSAL

We were actors
on life's stage,

Filled with sorrow,
fear and rage.

I played Hosea,
you played Gomer;

Set after set
you were a roamer.

Now it is time
to act again—

Stay close to me
through thick and thin,

For I said
to you, Amanda.

(Worthy of an
act much granda)

Although I sorrowed
for many a year,

And wondered if
you would ever hear,

May I call you
Amanda Renee?

(For desire is born
again each day)

Angels are watching—
there's no need to fear;

They've kept us safely
for many a year.

3/3/93

Amanda means worthy of love, and one meaning listed for Renee is born again. God has declared that each person is worthy of love, and can be born of the Spirit into new life. My sweetheart needed the assurance that she could start again in this life, that I had confidence in her desire and ability to live a different sort of life.

CONFRONTATION

Benoni was your grandchild;
   you wanted him to die.
You wouldn't let us keep him,
   or even tell us why.
You thought he'd die when he was born,
   but he was much too strong.
What ever gave you the right
   to help your wish along?
You never let us grieve the death
   that happened so long ago—
You beat me for trying to comfort her;
   how could you hate us so?
The baby wasn't even mine;
   his father's name was Joe,*
But I was ready to claim him,
   and eager to watch him grow.
He'd be a young man now—
   'twas nineteen seventy three,
And he would surely love you,
   had you shown him sympathy.

2/9/99

*Joe, as in "any old Joe". Although I believed I knew who had fathered her child, she was already traumatized by her encounter with him, and I thought giving him reason to interact with her in the future not wise.

When Benoni's grandmother was confronted with the ideas this poem sets forth, she stated simply, I don't remember any such events. Since then she has put a noticeable amount of effort to "prove" that these events could not have happened.

79

BUT I LOVED YOU

You murdered my children,

You threatened my young wife

That you'd stone her
    with a fork and a knife.

You poured out your hatred.

You laid it on quite thick,

Then you bashed my head
    with a hickory stick.

You said things against me;

Contemptuous words you let spew,

Then you whispered to others
    that I spoke evil of you.

When you were confronted

With charges against you,

You tried to smooth them over:
    "But I loved you!"

3/20/93

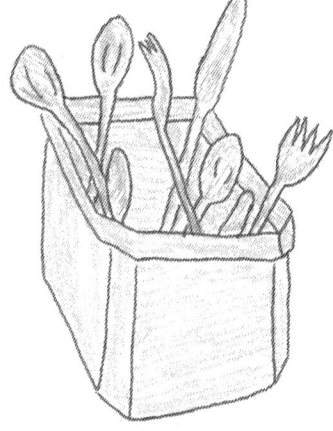

You are accusing me of things that never happened, she claimed.
I am innocent. Years have gone by, and she still clings to her claims that I am to blame for the unresolved differences between us. She also claims that I turned her daughter and grandchildren against her.

Jesus also had trouble forgiving those who crucified him. He cried out, Father, forgive them, for they know not what they do. The problem was not any failure or sin on His part. Some of the guilty individuals would not accept His forgiveness.

Can one rightly expect to be on terms of close friendship with God or with another person while rejecting such an essential part of friendship as resolving differences? I think not. Do we care enough to ask ourselves, "How do we call ourselves and others to repentance without passing judgement?"

WORK RECORDS

In case of emergency
    I now say,

Please try to contact
    Amanda Renee.

About loosing Janie
    I've no regret.

For her you need not
    worry or fret,

For the person to contact
    is the same,

Yet so diff'rent she deserved
    a new name.

So please write it down and
    rejoice with me,

For the Lord has given
    a great victory!

This poem is a slightly revised version of one composed 5/24/93.

* * * * * * * * * * * * * * * * * * * *
* * * * * * * * * * * * * * * * * *

How many different names has Amanda been called? To tell you the truth, I'll have to say I don't know. In this work several are mentioned; Maria Schneider, Wiggle Butt, Rahab, Janie Lou Hooker, to name a few. Some of the ones not included we don't even repeat in our household, because what they stand for as used in the past is too disgusting to us—connected to nothing positive, and loaded with sorrow for which there seems to be no resolution at present. If you find this multiplicity of names confusing, perhaps that will give you a glimpse of the confusion that has gone along with the turmoil and violence she has been put through, and why she wanted a name which stands for something positive.

SAD COMFORTERS

I heard a modern Bildad;
Come on, it's not that bad.
Just count your many blessings,
Then you won't feel so sad.
Don't spend your time in mourning,
Nor in making sad remarks;
Come on and do what Paul says—
Press forward toward the mark.
Think you not, Eliphaz,
They've been too long in grief;
If they'd praises instead of anger
That they might find relief?

        A terrible path they must have trod
        To so incur the wrath of God!
        Yes, I agree with you, Bildad;
        They must have done something bad.
        They surely must have provoked God,
        For He has struck them with His rod.

Like Job, we lost our children,
And all desire to live;
Now our worst tormenters
Deny the children ever lived.

Some things you must forget about,
Others tell me now;
Never stop to look back
When your hand is on the plow.

But if I don't look back,
How can I ever know
What it cost the God the Father
To redeem this world of woe?

How could I know Hosea's song
If I forgot the vow I made?
How could I treasure Jesus' love
If I forgot the price He paid?

6/3/93

PAINTING LIFESCAPES

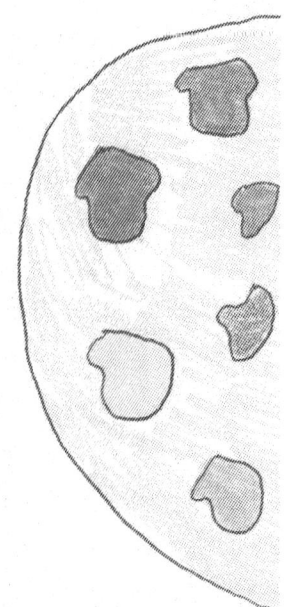

I am an artist,
    a poet, a musician,

Painting word pictures
    for the Great Physician.

I paint kindness
    on the canvas of life

In my dealings
    with my dear wife.

I paint forgiveness
    for many a foe,

Though they refuse
    my bold colors to know,

For I don't just paint
    in yellow and green;

Red, black, and blue
    on my canvas are seen.

When I paint truth,
    I include muddy gray,

For the grief of some things
    just won't go away.

I've long been learning
    Hosea's song—

That's why I paint
    with colors so strong.

7/2/93

83

REVELATION 17?

You heard about Doctor Jekyll
And his alter, Mister Hyde?
How he was a gentleman,
With a monster hidden inside?

But how about Doctor Heckle
And her secret, Sister Jive?
Beware least she deceive you;
She's very much alive.

She is a royal queen
For which I have no use;
Upon her mount she's been seen,
The beast we all call abuse.

If you knew what that woman
Has done to my sweet bride,
You would surely understan'
Why I ache inside.

7/27/93

In Revelation chapters 17 & 18, is God giving us an emotional word picture of His grief, as well as instruction and warning we need for the last days?

Ye adulterers an adulteresses, know ye not that the friendship of the world is enmity with God? Whosoever therefore will be a friend of the world is the enemy of God.

Submit yourselves therefore to God. Resist the devil, and he will flee from you.
Draw nigh to God, and he will draw nigh to you. Cleanse your hands, ye sinners; and purify your hearts, ye double minded. Be afflicted, and mourn, and weep: let your laughter be turned to mourning, and your joy to heaviness.

James 4: 4, 7-10.

TO TELL THE TRUTH

My heart is still full of tears
   When I think of that dreadful day,
      Though if has been twenty years
         Since Benoni passed away.

      The doctors wanted to save him,
         But the laws were not that kind;
            They backed his grandmother's whim,
               Putting the doctors in a bind.

            There legally was no father,
               Though 'tis said his name was Joe;
                  Because I was her best friend,
                     I shared his young mother's woe.

                  Sometimes I wish that I had lied
                     And given Benoni my last name,
                        For though to save him I surely tried,
                          The law said I had no right to claim.

8/10/93
in reference to
(8/19/73)

This poem is a statement about being subject to the same emotional reactions to trauma as everyone else. It is not about a desire to be dishonest, but a reference to the facet or stage of grief known as bargaining. Such emotional responses are not in and of themselves either good or bad, but they can open one up to temptation or to be taken advantage of by inconsiderate acquaintances. Logically I know I'm glad I did not lie. Had one person's bizarre behavior not taken over the sequence of events, Benoni would likely have survived. What happened was terrible, and his mother and I may not have been the only ones who were somehow never the same again for the experience.

COLORS OF GRIEF

Black is the color of Benoni's day;
On his day of birth he did pass away.
He was strong enough in this world to stay,
But someone his gift of life took away.

Blue is the mood of the hospital staff
As they shed their tears on his behalf;
In the law of the land there is a gaff
That tied the hands of the hospital staff.

Purple is the color of a wounded heart
In a young man willing to do his part,
And he was close to the mother's heart,
Though someone else Benoni's life did start.

Pink is the color of a protest sheet
To decry the loss of a life so sweet,
And to challenge a law so indiscreet
That wound allow loving hearts defeat.

Black is the color of Benoni's day,
Though twenty years have passed away,
For he lost his right to be here today,
To learn and love and work and play.

Composed 8/13/93
for use 8/19/93
(8/19/73)

Having showed a copy of this poem to my co-workers in the days between when it was composed and the date it commemorates, I went to work wearing black: Black shoes, black socks, black jeans, a black shirt, and a black and olive camouflage hat. I had black ribbon on my car, and out passed dark chocolate candy to anyone who would take it. Benoni's rights were trampled, destroyed, so perhaps the fact that no grave marker for him is to be found, only a brick inscribed with his name imbedded in a public sidewalk, where it too is walked on, matches the sad reality of his short life.

PRAYER OF DESPERATION

Father in Heaven,

I'm pacing the floor
In the midst of the night,
Boiling with anger,
And trembling with fright.

Memories of violence,
Of evil men's delight.
Pictures of a girl
To which they had no right.

Help me, oh Lord!
Revenge is in my heart.
Help me not now
From Thy path depart.
Comfort me, Lord,
And help me speak
Words which help others
Your truth to seek.
Help me to know
The dividing line
Between revenge
And justice fine.

Amen.

8/21/93

The event of the focus of this poem took place long before dawn one Sabbath morning. I awoke from a dream about certain men who took and sold indecent photographs, boiling with rage and a desire to go kill them. This is a record of my prayer. I was then able to have a peaceful and happy Sabbath.

REVELATION 3: 14—22?

Why, oh why, will you not confess?

Can you not see? Your life is a mess!

Laodocea, thou church of gloom,

Thou art like a whited tomb.

Repent, and your sins confess.

Though it turn your life to a mess,

It will bring a peace that will last;

Your confessed sins into the sea will be cast.

Behold, I knock on your door;

Your restoration I'm longing for.

All overcomers will sit at my throne,

Because for each sin I did atone.

8/22/93

One day I was lamenting to myself over those who let on that they are just fine, yet refuse to hear of charges against them. The specific ones I had in mind have declined to be forgiven, and in at least one case, have accused me of being unwilling to forgive. They want me to simply forget they have a problem so they can continue undisturbed, or so it seems. The question entered my mind, Is this what God is disgusted with, and saying so in portions of the messages to the seven churches?

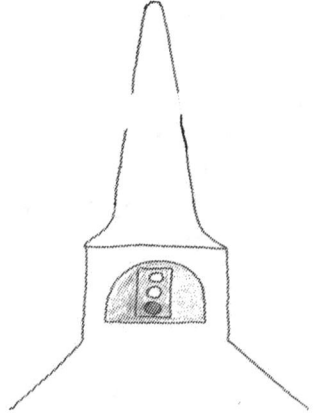

UNSEEN FRIEND

Our Savior is the unseen Friend

Upon whom all our hopes depend.

There is on earth no sweeter name

Than the precious name of Jesus.

He loved me and He knew my name

Before into the world I came.

He sends the Spirit to tend the flame

Of love that burns for His name.

There is no other Friend on earth

Who can give us hope without an end.

Lord, help me understand the worth

Of the precious name of Jesus.

3/31/93

Lewis E. Miles

THE PRICE HE PAID

Great drops of blood He sweat that night
      in Gethsemane.
As He prayed, "Father, let this cup pass from me,
      but Thy will be done.

In the distance He could hear the howling mob
      coming after Him, coming after Him.

He soared above it all that night;
      His decision had been made.
He'd save man from his fallen state
      by dying on a tree.

He stirs up the people and makes them shout
That He will be ruler and we will be out.
He's guilty of high treason and blasphemy—
Let's take him and nail him to a tree!

They shoved Him and beat Him and spat in His face
But He was so burdened He scarce felt the pain
That tortured Him, - - - - that taunted Him.
His heartache was the greatest pain He felt—
the weight of the sins He bore.
That's what really hurt our Lord;
the weight of your shame and mine.

1977

He is despised and rejected of men; a man of sorrows, and acquainted with grief: and we hid as it were our faces from him; he was despised, and we esteemed him not. Surely he hath borne our griefs, and carried our sorrows: yet we did esteem him stricken, smitten of God, and afflicted. But he was wounded for our transgressions, he was bruised for our iniquities: the chastisement of our peace was upon him; and with his stripes we are healed.

Isaiah 53:3-6

IN RETROSPECT

I spoke a message in sixty eight
That's been bearing fruit of late.

Don't punish your children for their fright,
Though they disobey with all their might,
For characters are not refined that way;
From God you'll turn their hearts away.
They need someone who's all heart and ears
To care and listen to their fears.

The teachers came to me one day,
We'd like your help again today,
For one of our students has disappeared;
We know not where she is or what she fears.

A test of my theory began that day;
Some may still think that I was wrong,
For her confusion was very strong.
Time after time she went astray;
My glimmer of hope 'bout faded away,
But now I have no cause for dismay,
For she's heard me calling, "Amanda Renee".
(You are truly worthy of love,
And to be born again from above.)

9/30/93

The Lord hath appeared of old unto me, saying,
Yea, I have loved thee with an everlasting love:
therefore with loving kindness have I drawn thee.
Jeremiah 31:3

He hath shewed thee, O man, what is good; and what
doth the Lord require of thee, but to do justly, and
to love mercy, and to walk humbly with thy God.
Micah 6:8

None of us can match the loving kindness of God,
or the mercy He shows to each one of us. This fact,
more than anything else, I have learned in my effort
to show kindness and mercy to my beloved.

Section Four

Samples of Hosea's

coping mechanisms

and early philosophy

BEEP BEEP!

When I was growing up, Roadrunner was my favorite cartoon. I just loved the way that, however hard he tried, Wiley Coyote never got much over on Roadrunner. If Roadrunner got tired, he'd do something like stop, throw up a wall, and paint a tunnel on it. Just as Mr. Coyote came upon him, he'd step through the tunnel, but Mr. Coyote would splatter himself on the wall. Each episode, however different, had similar results.

As early in life as age seven or eight I had a rudimentary understanding of the concept of the workings of memory and recall by association or dissociation. I identified with Roadrunner, and associated Wiley Coyote with my worst foe at the time, my grandfather. Although he was violent to me, psychologically it seemed that when I felt desperate, I'd always splatter him on the wall.

One time he caught me squealing on him on the phone and beat me over the head with a cane until I fell to the floor, then proceeded to kick me violently. I never felt much pain from that, but three days later he was still complaining about his foot hurting. That's what you get for kicking someone tougher than you are, I taunted him.

(Matt. 25:40 & 45, Acts 9:5)

After I caught him sexually abusing a male relative when I was ten, his response was to "get even" by abusing me. Because, however, I had received some instructions from the one I'd caught him abusing, I was prepared to make a show of resistance, then pretend to change my mind. I got him involved, then got my revenge, turning the emotional tables on him. In the end, he was the one who ran out of the pantry screaming. I laughed and said, "serves you right, you old fool."

When I suspected he was trying to poison me, I poured the liquid he'd given me to drink out by the back door, which was near the well. Soon afterwards someone found dead chickens by the back door, at the base of the steps where I had poured the drink. I had not left the house except to pour out the liquid. For some time after that he wouldn't drink the water from his well, but hauled it in bottles. I laughed every time I offered him a drink of water. Everyone else drinks it, I told him. What's wrong with you, are you a chicken?

Because, he claimed, mom and I had both broken secrecy, and I had gone beyond defending myself to talk about his abuse of others, his criminal activities, and his ties to the Chicago mob, he later molested my sister. My response was to talk even more, and to make sure he didn't get his job back, the one he had used as a front until I squealed on him. I laughed when he accused me of being responsible for his financial troubles.

Knowing as I did of his promise to get me some day, and understanding that one of his sons had lost a fiancée after bringing her to meet the family because she went off and committed suicide, I'd have never taken an "innocent girl" there and STAYED OVERNIGHT. Instead of having sought out the most stable, well balanced girl I could find, I had brought one of whom it was said by the time she was eleven, "no one will ever settle that girl down". I told her about my expectations, and even though I suggested that she either come crawl in with me or that I take her somewhere else to sleep, she decided not to make a scene.

He came up the stairs in the middle of the night, waved his pistol at me, went to her and made a couple of quiet commands as he was waking her up. She rolled over, pushed her pants down, and spread her legs. She even smiled at him before he raped her, realizing that might lessen the violence against her.

In the morning he taunted me. That girl won't want to marry you now, and you won't want her, but you'll have to marry her. I feigned ignorance. What do you mean by that, I asked? What are you, stupid, he exclaimed! I probably got her pregnant for you, knowing my record. So, I replied, smirking, do you think that would be the first time? Her mother killed all the other babies. I didn't bring someone who is going to react like the one your middle son brought. He got quite noticeably nervous. I continued, You made a fool out of yourself last night, I continued. You didn't need that pistol. All you needed to do was ask her. I took advantage of his obvious shock at what I'd just said by adding more, just to throw his emotional control farther off balance.

How'd you like the prostitute I brought with me?

Somehow, Wiley Coyote just knew he was about to hit the wall again, but he just wouldn't give up the contest. When I asked the question, "How'd you like the prostitute I brought?", I could see him brace his emotional feet and start to skid. "I could have brought another one, but then it would have been too obvious." Splat! Then I stepped out from behind the wall and said, "Beep Beep!" By the way, whadya catch from her? Then I ground it in some more. I won't say much if you promise not to blow my cover. Is that a deal? Ya? I'd offer to shake on it, but as you remember, I promised I'd never shake with you unless it was the kiss of Judas, and I haven't forgotten. Neither have your bosses' "sons". The next night he came upstairs again, minus the pistol, mumbling something as he came about how he wished he'd known how simple it would have been. Why'd they have to make such a scene? He groped around in the dark, but she was not there on the floor by the door. When he got to the bed in the room and started to check it out, the cousin who was in it bashed him on the head with a baseball bat. He hollered and swore. People came running, half asleep.

What's the big idea, someone demanded? I don't know, he replied. All I was doing was looking for that girl that stupid grandson of mine brought. Where is she anyhow? Their anger slowly gave way to anxiety when they couldn't find her either, even with the hall light on. I got up and went down to the bathroom, meeting him at the bottom of the stairs. "It's about time you got up," he growled. You better help find your girlfriend. I'm not worried about it, I replied airily. That's your problem You remember what I said, and you'll know what I mean. The wall falls on him and smashes Wiley Coyote flat.

I relieved myself and went back up to bed. As soon as I slid into the huge pile of quilts, she hugged me fiercely under the covers. Mom came over and asked, "How come you won't help look?" I'm not worried about it, I replied. Does that mean you know where she is, she asked? Yes, she's right here with me, I answered. I was wondering about that, mom stated. Under the circumstances I guess it will have to be ok. I couldn't help it. My choked off laugh came out as a snort. Beep Beep! See you again next show.

MY LEARNING PROCESS

When I stated in "BEEP BEEP!" that I had a rudimentary understanding of the functions of memory and recall by association and dissociation by the time I was seven or eight, I did not mean that I used those terms, which I didn't encounter until several years later. Rather, I thought in terms of linking ideas and memories together like one links Tinkertoy pieces. A few such pieces were in the toy collection at my grandparents' place, and I used them to think through the construction of a model of mental function. Fear, or more specifically, terror, I saw as being like a connecting socket plugged by a broken off connector, or like a bit of hardened clay clogging the socket so the bit of information couldn't be linked to other ideas besides fear. The greater the number of sockets which became clogged, the harder future recall would be. An unlinked piece might, so to speak, fall through the register, making retrieval extremely difficult, if not impossible. Conversely, retrieving and reviewing a memory was like connecting the piece on more ways, making it larger and easier to keep track of. By the age of ten, I had included rage and substance abuse with terror as blocking agents. Today I might call them triggers for dissociation.

Although I had begun to formulate questions before that, at age five I began to spend time and mental energy trying to figure out why people, particularly my paternal grandmother, had trouble remembering simple things. I questioned her patiently, and discovered and confirmed that there was a link between her fears and compulsions and her forgetfulness.

My model which used the toy as a visual aide steered me toward an answer about what to do if fear plugged a connecting socket. Hurry to connect another idea, thought, or emotion before the fear or rage could curl around like a pretzel and block all the controlled access to the event. Humor was the tool I found most effective, particularly if based on word play or deliberately constructed visual imagery. I called the latter imagination. Use these quickly, and a potential abuser's power is greatly reduced. They tended to move on and look for easier targets. If they returned, they discovered that I remembered things they didn't want to be reminded of, and hoped I would have forgotten.

Along with that, I discovered that the thinking processes of most abusive persons leave them vulnerable. Much as a thief or an embezzler seeks the easy way out, an abusive person tends toward a sort of mental laziness. They skip steps of logic, fail to check and countercheck what they have thought through, hoping to get what they want quickly and easily. Jumping to conclusions doesn't result in efficient mental function. Wear them out, exhaust them by giving them more chances to jump to conclusions than they can handle, and they will likely move on.

The achievement of personal power enables one to show compassion to victims of abuse, and sometimes even the abusers, by showing them kindness and helping them deal with some of the emotional blockages (fear, rage, etc.) that helped set the abuse situation up or gave it lasting power over them.

The resource which has proved to be the most valuable to me in gaining understanding has been the Bible, the holy book of Christianity. Even if you are not a Christian, I invite you to investigate the warning against child abuse found in Exodus 20:5&6. Compare the fourth chapter of Hosea with Revelation chapters seventeen and eighteen to see a description of the parallelism between the effects of sexual abuse and drunkenness in their devastating, dissociating effects.

The book of Hosea teaches that recovery is possible, and that the most generous attributes of love are what lead the way—kindness and patience.

Do those ideas make sense? The Bible's portrayal of the ideas of the intrinsic value of each individual seem to be timeless, as does its teaching of tactful confrontation linked with affirmation.

Q & A

Q In the battle over abortion, who is right?

A Those who believe in doing justly, who love mercy, and who walk humbly with their God. Walking humbly with God means to diligently seek His answer to each decision in life.

Q Who is clearly out of place?

A Those who fight violence with violence. Those with judgmental attitudes, or who refuse to forgive. Those who ignore Matthew 7:12.

Q Are the pro choice people correct in saying that abortion is not mentioned in the Bible?

A Yes, and no. The word abortion is not in any of the versions in my possession, but study before saying the subject is not covered. Some of the following texts may be helpful:

Exodus 13: 2, 21:22, 34:19&20. Deuteronomy 28:1-4. Ruth 4:13.
I Samuel 15:33. II Samuel 11:5. II Kings 8:12. Job 3:11&16.
Psalm 127:3-5. Proverbs 6:16-19. Ecclesiastes 6:3. Isaiah 49:1, 57:3-5. Hosea
13:16. Micah 6:6-8. Romans 9:11. I Timothy 2:5.

Q What is symbolized by the beast of Revelation chapter 17?

A Does anything fit better as a definition of this symbol than abuse of power?

Q What is forgiveness?

A Forgiveness is both a gift and a transaction. Each of us is issued a blank check for complete forgiveness, but it is up to each of us to take our own freely given gift to the bank of memory and confession to cash or redeem it. In our dealings with fellow humans, much prayer and study is needed. I believe that only God can show us the proper balance of openness and restraint. (see Matt. 10:8, 7:6, 10:16, and James 5:16)

Q Can pro life and pro choice adherents be equally wrong?

A Yes. Either or both can be motivated by the wrong spirit.

Q In the hour of His judgement depicted in Revelation 14:12, who is on trial? Who is the prosecutor, who is the jury, and who are the witnesses? What does that mean to us?

A In the great conflict over rulership of the universe, God is the defendant, prosecuted by Lucifer, (the devil or dragon) who claims to have equal rights of rulership. He claims that God is not really just or merciful, but rules out of self serving interests at the expense of his subjects. Humans, having had opportunity to experience the results of the plans of both contestants, are the primary witnesses. All the unfallen beings are the jurors, deciding on the basis of the evidence brought forth by the witnesses. Each potential witness is screened to determine whether they will desire to give a true testimony, or to cherish deceitfulness and abuse of power.

Q Does the statement in Revelation 21:4, "God shall wipe away all tears... for the former things are passed away" mean that God will erase our memories, taking something away from us?

A No. Recall of memory will be completely restored; nothing will be blocked from our recall by fear and confusion. Every conflict will be resolved, and every memory freed into the accessible knowledge of the individual. The charge of Lucifer that God is arbitrary and withholds that which would empower will be shown for the cruel and abusive lie that it is.

Q What about Isaiah 26:14, which states that God made all memory to perish?

A When read in context, this passage seems to be a statement about man's condition in death. Ecclesiastes 9:5 puts it this way; "The living know they shall die, but the dead know not anything." God is merciful. He does not add to the agony of the faithful witnesses by taking them straight to heaven to have to endure watching the continued suffering of their loved ones. In His mercy, He leaves them "in the grave" until the resurrection. At that time He will gather them to receive their reward.

He will help them resolve all personal conflict, and answer any questions which remain about the justice of the final decisions.

Q Why are some "condemned to hell" if God desires to save all.

A God is not arbitrary; He allows free choice even at the expense of His own comfort. Those who refuse to do the grief processing work (even if absolute safety were guaranteed) of going to the bank of memory and confession to cash their checks of forgiveness would never be happy in Heaven or on the Earth made new. They will choose death rather than the completion of this work, so God will sadly and regretfully give them the desire of their hearts, so as not to prolong their misery.

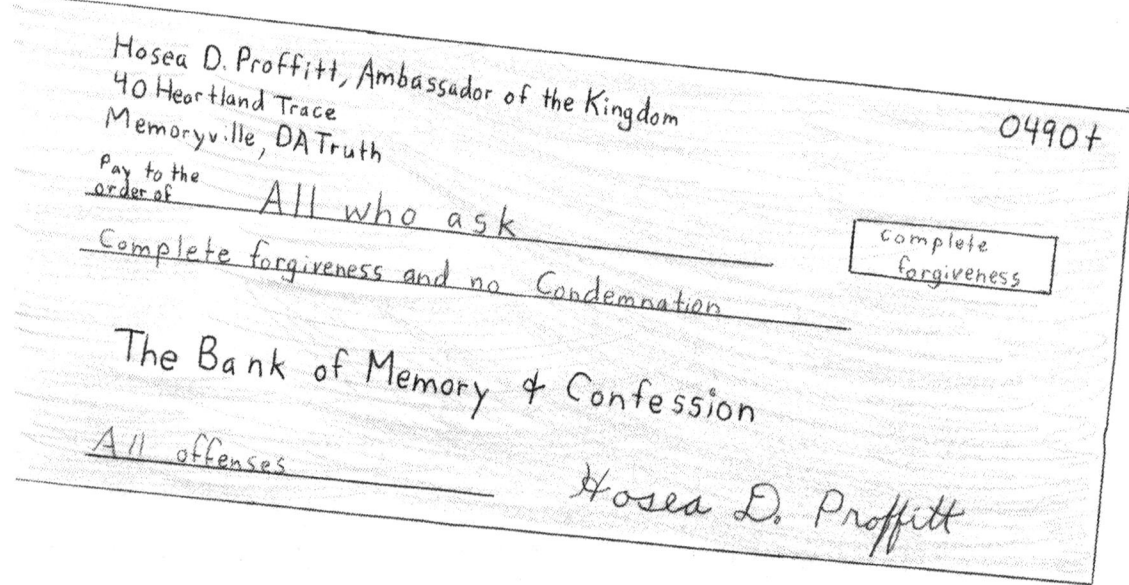

Q Can any man absolve sin?

A No. We can, however, pass on the wonderful news of God's wonderful promise of forgiveness. The holy spirit can empower us to be fit ambassadors for the kingdom of God.

THE RIGHT CHOICE?

Why do I feel so weary,	She's no good anyhow, they say,
Why is my heart so sad?	She wouldn't treat them right.
Why are my thoughts so dreary,	Her whole life's in disarray,
Why is my heart not glad?	They howl with great delight.
I mourn for the loss of children	She's done what she was taught
And for the destruction of trust	Throughout her childhood days,
By those whose actions bewilderin'	And though her heart's overwrought,
Are driven by their sick lust.	She knows not diff'rent ways.
Cry out for all the Benonis!	They pass around her photographs
Weep again for slain Abigail!	And laugh about her naked shame;
Mourn on for all the agonies;	If in the act they should get caught
The train of justice has been derailed.	On her they'd place the blame.
A death sentence for their innocence,	Oh people, can you hear me
And torture for their mother's heart.	Above the revelers dreadful roar?
The strong come not to their defense	Please listen to my heart's plea
Nor take their death to heart.	And add not confusion more.
No marker for their memory,	Go not to war for abortion
No record of their short life.	And clamor not for choice,
No record of the bitter agony	Nor make pro-life your choice
Of the ones who gave them life.	With tones of angry voice.
There's laughter in the darkness-	For there's no justice without kindness,
The sound of a jeering voice	And no mercy without restraint.
Deriding the poor mother's weakness	Our words are full of emptiness
As a good reason to rejoice.	If they bear hatred's taint.

11/5/95

Is the child a Benoni—"a son (or daughter) of my sorrow", or an Abigail—"the joy of the father"? Should that determine the right to life or the lack of it? I think not. Does that determine whether or not the mother feels anguish over the child's demise? Evidence indicates that the grief is there regardless. What about the father—is he unaffected?

In the cases I have become aware of, he grieves too, and may have a harder time finding an acceptable outlet.

In those days they shall say no more, the fathers have eaten a sour grape, and the children's teeth are set on edge. But every one shall die for his own iniquity: every man that eateth the sour grape, his teeth shall be set on edge. Jeremiah 31:29&30

101

Lewis E. Miles

Section Five

Reflections, Judgements, and Warnings.

ANSWERING ATHALIAH

Her cry...........If what you say is true,
　　　　　　I was an awful criminal
　　　　　　With a distorted view,
　　　　　　And he a wimp dismal.

My reply.........He was not a wimp,
　　　　　　I want to shout,
　　　　　　But what I remember
　　　　　　Bears your claim out,
　　　　　　For though he'd always listen,
　　　　　　To the sadness of my heart,
　　　　　　It still makes my eyes glisten,
　　　　　　For he failed to do his part
　　　　　　To protect children form abuse,
　　　　　　Even when it was pointed out;
　　　　　　To act tough he did refuse,
　　　　　　Allowing precious lives snuffed out.

Reflections......Is it always wrong to threaten?
　　　　　　Is it unhealthy to scream?
　　　　　　Is forgivin' and forgettin'
　　　　　　Always what it seems?

　　　　　　He has shown you,
　　　　　　O man, what is good;
　　　　　　(To stop the carnage
　　　　　　You really should.)
　　　　　　To love mercy
　　　　　　(Even for the unborn child)
　　　　　　And to do justly
　　　　　　(Let not your hands be defiled)
　　　　　　And to walk humbly with the Lord.
　　　　　　(Not doing the things He's abhorred)

1/30/94

And thou saidst, I shall be a lady for ever: so thou didst not lay these things to heart, neither didst remember the latter end of it.

Therefore hear now this, thou that art given to pleasures, that dwelleth carelessly, that sayest in thine heart, I am, and none else beside me; I shall not as a widow, neither shall I know the loss of children:

But these two things shall come to thee in a moment in one day, the loss of children, and widowhood: they shall come upon thee in their perfection for the multitude of thy sorceries, and for the great abundance of thine enchantments. Isaiah 47: 7—9

BEYOND CHAPTER THREE

I started my research back when I was five,

And I'm still trying to sort out the jive.

Some say my stories are all contrived,

Or imagination took me for a drive.

Can I visit your house, and talk to the walls,

And from their soft whispers a story recall?

I need no money when on you I call—

My reputation will pay for it all.

Some think I'm crazy, but that's ok;

Never expect everyone to heed what you say.

Don't let them tell you that I'm keeping score;

Truth and kindness are all I ask for.

2/15/94 & 5/1/01

For it is written, I will destroy the wisdom of the wise,
and will bring to nothing the understanding of the prudent.
Where is the wise? where is the scribe? where is the
disputer of this world? 1 Corinthians 1: 19 & 20

If any of you lack wisdom, let him ask of God, that giveth
to all men liberally, and upbraideth not; and it shall be
given him. But let him ask in faith, nothing wavering.
For he that wavereth is like a wave of the sea driven
with the wind and tossed. James 1: 5 & 6

HOSEA'S JUDGEMENT

Dear _____,

Some people hold grudges; others realize that character development is a learning process, and do not judge others by their past errors, but by what they have overcome.

To illustrate what this means, one could draw this analogy; if a person bathes regularly and does not in general smell objectionable, should we condemn them for having once been so excessively filthy that when they went swimming they left a ring in the lake? I think not.

Sincerely,
Hosea

Why does Revelation 22:11 say something that sounds unforgiving? Doesn't "and he that is filthy, let him be filthy still" sound harsh, unmerciful, and unforgiving? Why would God, who "is faithful and just to forgive us our sins, and to cleanse us from all unrighteousness" say such a thing? The answer lies in the very nature of forgiveness. Forgiveness is a transaction, as well as a gift. If the intended recipient is unwilling to cash the gift at the bank of memory and confession, the transaction will never be completed, the gift never received. When no one exists who is willing to complete the transaction, God will make that proclamation.

The above letter was not sent to one longtime adversary, Vivian Athaliah Hooker, because sending it would likely do no good. She has already turned down countless offers of forgiveness, and now says, "I am innocent." As far as I'm concerned, her probation with me is closed—she, short of a miracle from God, will never be my friend here on this earth.

I am not God, of course, and cannot know the future as he does, and this is not to be considered an eternal proclamation.

God alone can make that decision.

Lewis E. Miles

WHAT'S YOUR PLEA?

You said you've been an awful grinch,
But you have yet to feel the pinch
That you deserve for what you've done;
To talk your sister has begun.
She talks 'bout Cloudland Canyon Point,
And being held by ankle joint;
Of being raped and treated rough
In broad daylight out on the bluff,
Then suff'ring from indignity;
Being tied naked to a tree.
Talks about Reflection Riding
And dark secrets that you're hiding;
Of how you left her there all night,
With no companion but a snake,
Which wiggled with ev'ry move she'd make.
Says you took her to UTC
And raped her there for all to see,
Than repeated it for your dad,
To show him how much "fun" she had.
It was no fun for her at all
To answer to your beck and call,
Terrified she might just croak
Next time you decided to choke.
She talks of horrors in the night,
How you disrespected her rights
To sleep peacefully in her own room;
'Cause your dad failed to drop the boom
And prosecute you for the crime,
You did it time after time.

You've hurt her much more recently
Down here in Orangeburg and Santee.
Choking her in the discount store,
Making her look like a crude whore
Who'd drop her clothes there in the aisle
And let her kids watch all the while.
Too soon after she'd given birth,
You hated her for all you're worth,
Forcing her time after time,
Adding insults to your crimes.
For weeks she continued to bleed,
But to her pain you gave no heed,
Shoving your threats into her head,
Letting her believe she'd be dead
If she opened her mouth to talk,

So against you she made no squawk.
Too long you've had your way like this;
Don't come again round your sis,
Thumbing your nose at all the laws.
It's time prosecution you saw.

3/22/94

Lewis E. Miles

AN ACROSTIC WARNING

Know ye who this is talking to;
Understand to whom it is due.
Now's the time for al to repent;
Give your whole heart to a new bent.

Forcing others against their will,
Using fear to keep their lips still,
Enjoying taunting those who care;
Your conscience should bring you despair.

In your heart there has been no good,
So plead for mercy like you should.

Your deeds are known to other men;
Others still want you in a pen.
Up til now you've thought you're immune -
Repent, for justice cometh soon!

Never mind the vengeance of man;
Answer to God while you still can.
Make confession to God and man:
Enter into his blessed plan.

3/25/94

CRYINGDALE ACADEMY

Start crying in the office,
Begin weeping in the halls,
For dreadful things have happened,
And we each must face them all.

Because you valued honor
More than you did the truth,
You neglected your duty
To stand firm 'gainst things uncouth.

I spoke about a darkroom
And gross things that happened there.
 We can't check out your rumor—
 To him we must be fair.
The girls you showed no mercy,
And their foe no justice fair—
No good you did to either;
They thought you didn't care.

Cry to the Lord for mercy,
And for your sins shed a tear,
For grievous is God's anger,
And judgement draweth near.

Start crying in the office,
Begin weeping in the halls,
Cry out to the Lord for mercy,
And heed the Spirit's call.

It's time all learn the lesson;
It is time to see the truth,
For we must do our duty,
So be sure to know the truth.
If any lack for wisdom,
Then let him cry out to God,
For can He judge us guiltless
If we withhold the rod?

What teach we about our God
If we all ignore abuse?

111

Will any of the victims
Believe His love is profuse?
And what of the aggressor
Who no one bothers to bust?
How will he ever learn that
We serve a God who is just?

Start crying in the office,
Begin weeping in the halls,
Cry to the Lord for mercy,
And heed the Spirit's call.

3/29/94

LAMENT FOR GRASSY VALE

Cry out to the Lord, o thou Grassy Vale;
Cry out loud to the Lord, and weep and wail.
Cry out with much anguish, and grow pale:
To heed children's anguish, you did long fail.
The laws of Moses you gave little heed—
The laws of the land you gave little heed—
To do as they wished did your men proceed,
Ignoring the safety young people need.
Your men treated girls as they did a wife,
Your sons took your daughters midst scenes of strife,
Even when promised to someone for life.
Your lack of justice in our day was rife.
Cry out loud, o people who claim to love
All of the message that came from above,
Yet under the rug their troubles did shove,
By choosing death instead of love,
Who destroyed our children like garden weeds.
To medicine's high places you did speed,
Thinking abortion relieved a great need,
And to our great anguish gave little heed.
Cry out to the Lord, o thou vale of grass;
A cry to your God from your lips let pass,
For your worship was as a sounding brass,
And too soon for you His judgement will pass.
The girls were not safe in your slackened hand;
You strove not to stop the things God has banned.
You let the evil ones do just as they'd planned,
For no respect from them did you command.
Cry out to the Lord, o thou vale of gloom;
Cry out to the Lord, ere you meet your doom.
Cry out for your children snatched from the womb;
Weep for dead babies who entered no tomb.
Too long you spent building far out of plumb;
Your house will topple when the great storms come.
A much hated place will this vale become,
And your defenders will be struck dumb.
Cry out to the Lord, o thou Grassy Vale,
Cry out to the Lord, and weep and wail.
Cry out with much anguish, and grow pale,
Least in the final test, you not prevail.

3/29 & 30/94

113

THE EIGHTH DAY

They meet upon the mountain top,

They gather in the park.

They're righteous until sundown,

But madman after dark.

Now for the entertainment;

They're sure you'll think it fun,

But it will turn your stomach

Ere it is halfway done.

They say it is an illusion,

But it is all too real,

Yet they claim delusion

When someone tries to squeal.

Come out of this my people,

I hear the angel cry—

The final time of decision

Is swiftly drawing nigh.

O faithful ones in Israel,

Be careful what you say;

Deal kindly with God's children,

And grieve them not away.

9/28/94

THE VOICES OF GOMER'S STRUGGLE

I hear them calling from the mountain top—
What's wrong with you, that to him you gave in?
Why did you let him convince you to stop?
What's all this nonsense 'bout how mean we've been?
We all know you well; you are one of us,
So come on up and enjoy life again!
Let that grouchy ol' prophet sit and fuss.
You need not sit and suffer with your pain!

I feel it strongly now, the urge to go,
To be again the center of it all,
But I remember now, and so I know—
There's much danger in answering their call.

It is late at night—shall I just slip out?
"Let's go!", I hear my inner voices scream.
I slip on my robe, I map out my route,
Yet I linger in the doorway to dream.
Like a great specter, the memories come—
Scenes of murder on the mountain at night;
Adults, and babies whose time is not come.
I'm stiff as a statue, frozen with fright,
For fear that I may never come back,
Yet voices still call me into the night.
I want to stay, but my resolve is slack.
I slip out the door, pause in the dark,
And turn to gaze at Hosea's prayer light.
I turn back toward that love kindled spark
And cry out, "Hosea, please hold me tight!"

9/2/94

THE DROPOUT

Deep is her depression.
Ominous is her grief.
Intense is her sorrow,
With never any relief.

This kind requires much fasting and prayer;
What did you while I was up there?

Come out of him, and enter no more!
Thrashing, writhing, screaming, then limp on the floor;
Of no use seem'd our Lord's command,
'Til He lifted him and helped him stand.

Thou shalt abide with me many a day,
And no longer the harlot you will play.
For many days without thoughts for a king,
No joy to your heart could society bring.
Not to ritual, nor to God's Temple come;
By confusion and grief too overcome.
Money shall be worthless in your hand,
Too overcome with grief to understand.

Abide like this for many days,
Then you shall enter the house of praise.

5/21/95

This poem is a reflection of Hosea 3:3-5, Mark 9:17-29, and the personal observations of the author of this work.

In the ninth chapter of the Gospel of John is told the story of Jesus healing a man born blind. Woven into the story is an indication of the abuse of authority by the religious leaders of that day. They had declared that whoever proclaimed that Jesus was the Christ should be put out of the synagogue. Even some of the leaders believed, according to chapter 12:42&43, but they could not prevail against men determined to uphold the traditions that protected their positions.

Is it possible that modern spiritual leaders are in danger of taking a stand against the work of the Holy Spirit and the call out of Babylon recorded in Revelation 18:14? Does the danger exist that by rejecting the contemporary abuse survivor recovery movement we might reject the call out of Babylon?

A TIME OF TROUBLE

Kung Fuey's sadistic attack,
The bittersweet gift of a life,
Bringing all the dread issues back
For me and my poor hurting wife.
I will not force her, and I wonder,
Has she the strength to pass the test,
Or will she 'gain knuckle under
And do what God says is not best?
A time for us of great weeping
And staggering from our great pain.
A time of prayer vigils keeping,
Least we should see folly again.
How long, o great tribulation,
Will you rain on us from your vial?
How long with great trepidation
Must we carry on all the while?
How long must we toil in darkness,
How long must we wrestle at night?
Forsake us not in our weakness;
O Lord, give us strength to do right.

Come back, o heart from bad dreamland,
Look away now from your sad fears;
Gods deliverance understand,
And into His presence draw near.

    O search your heart, Kung Fuey,
    One last time I'm calling to you.
    Come forth with your full repentance
    While there's still time left for you.

Hold up your head, Amanda,
Be bold to look them in the eye.
Your fears they can now understand—
Now surely it's their time to cry;
They have no strength to meet your gaze,
And sense a need to view their shoes.
They babble with a foolish craze
Before you begin to accuse.
They try to stay away from you,
But see you standing in the hall—
They turn to flee away from you,
And crash right into the glass wall.

Be careful how you speak to them,
For I desire them for my friends;
On how you present me to them
The outcome of many depends.

4/11/94

A CRY OF JOY

Come now, my good and faithful bride,

With joy I call you to my side,

For you've been faithful to your vow,

Although others do not see how

I could ever say such a thing,

For well known are your many flings.

I saw the desire of your heart,

And you were faithful from the start

To keep the simple vow you made;

Judgment in your favor has been made,

And your portion ever will be

To live and rejoice here with me.

4/26/94

Hosea—a savior, or salvation. We are created in the image of God, who alone can save or restore. To reflect His image, however, we must reflect His restoring, redeeming qualities. The devil is the destroyer.

God is the creator and restorer. Who do you wish to reflect?

Then thou shalt call, and the Lord shall answer; thou shalt cry, and He shall say, Here I am. If thou take away from the midst of thee the yoke, the putting forth of the finger, and speaking vanity; ~ ~ ~ the Lord shall guide thee continually, ~ ~ ~ and thou shalt be called, The repairer of the breach, The restorer of paths to dwell in. Taken from Isaiah 58:9,11,&12.

Lewis E. Miles

ABOUT THE AUTHOR

Lewis Miles is a truck driver and sometimes poet who has lived in South Carolina, USA, for the past fifteen years. His years of study and reflection on what the Book of Hosea and other portions of the Christian Bible say about abuse issues found in modern society blossomed into this collection of poetry and prose, most of which he recorded in the 1990s.

He likes to spend his free time with his family, attends church regularly, and enjoys participating in quiet hobbies like bird watching, die cast car collecting, and reading. His favorite sport is NASCAR, his favorite personal vehicle is one that is both paid for and dependable, and his favorite book, other than the Bible, at the moment is this one, because he has put so much into it. One of his children once said his main occupation is being silly, but as can be seen in this work, there is a sensitive and serious side to him as well.